THE ASSISTANT

New Tasks, New Opportunities

THE ASSISTANT

New Tasks, New Opportunities

Elizabeth R. Murphy

amacom
A Division of American Management Associations

To my husband,
who knew I could do it
before I did

Library of Congress Cataloging in Publication Data

Murphy, Elizabeth R.
The assistant—new tasks, new opportunities.

Bibliography: p.
Includes index.
1. Secretaries. I. Title.
HF5547.6.M87 651.3′741 81-69370
ISBN 0-8144-5675-8 AACR2

First Printing

CONTENTS

INTRODUCTION

Today's assistant is at a career crossroads. Because of the rapid introduction of word processing equipment, because of the emphasis in organizations on individual productivity, because of the diminishing view of the secretary as a status symbol, the assistant to a manager today is performing a different job than yesterday's secretary did.

What was a traditional secretary, and how is today's assistant different? In the past, a secretary was expected to be an extension of her boss, an appendage, a responder to his needs alone. Today the assistant is more often in charge of whole areas of the department's work, and her value is seen in her ability to take independent, self-initiated action. Yesterday's secretary was often a symbol—a manifestation of the success of her manager, similar to the furniture in his office and other trappings related to his level in the organization. Today's assistant is expected to be as results oriented as any other member of the management team. Formerly, a secretary was judged primarily by her skills in such technical aspects of the job as typing and shorthand. Today the assistant may have others (or machines) to do much of this work, leaving her free to think, plan, and make improvements.

Many assistants reading this book may find it difficult to identify with my concept of an assistant. But that doesn't mean the book isn't relevant for them. Even though many secretaries have not yet moved away from the traditional role, there is a definite trend in organizations to that type of change.

This trend is similar to what we see in the changing face of management itself. The old-style traditional manager was authoritarian and action oriented and very often worked independently of others. The "today" manager involves his people, uses human relations techniques, and increasingly takes time to plan. That doesn't mean there are no more traditional managers. It means that more and more managers tend to be of the "newer" type, and fewer and fewer tend to be traditional. Just so, there are still traditional secretaries, but they are gradually giving way to today's more independent and self-propelled assistant. This book is a preparation for that change.

WHY THE BOOK WAS WRITTEN

I am in the business of management training. Each year I conduct approximately 35 seminars to train about 1,000 people—managers, supervisors, and assistants—in management skills. In working with assistants over the past five years, I have developed teaching materials to give them the skills and attitudes they need to do their jobs. I've also had a chance to find out their problems, their hopes, and their needs. All the material in this book comes from my seminar experience with assistants.

I have always found it difficult to find good material to recommend to assistants for reading after the seminar. I found myself saying: "There aren't any books that address today's assistant." I said it so much that I decided to write one myself.

A number of different kinds of people will find this book useful. Organizations are beginning to see the worth of sending assistants out to training seminars, but there are still many who have never had the opportunity to have any formal training. Those assistants can use this book in lieu of training. The others can use this book to build on their training and help them apply their new knowledge. Women who are considering getting back into the workforce after time spent at home will find this book an orientation to today's work world. Students in the secretarial sciences will find the book useful in enhancing the "reality" aspects of their study.

TODAY'S ASSISTANTS

The assistants I have taught had many titles: secretary, personal secretary, executive secretary, administrative assistant, administrative secretary, assistant to, assistant supervisor, office assistant, and a few others as well. Some of their problems and characteristics were unique, but most were similar. These are some of my observations on assistants as a group:

- They perform many different kinds of jobs. Some of them are traditional "go-fers"; others are doing managerial-level work.
- They are frustrated. Although some assistants are quite happy in their jobs, many still find it difficult to be included as part of the management team, and they don't want to be somebody's "girl" any more.
- They are competent. For the most part, the assistants I meet are performing a vital function in their company and doing it well. It is fascinating, in a seminar, to hear their good ideas on making improvements in their jobs, their departments, and their organizations.
- They often feel pulled in two directions. Even those who want to advance into higher management have to deal with the pressures of those around them to stay in their places and be everybody's idea of a "nice lady." Because the assistant used to be seen as a not-too-bright phone answerer, she has to work even harder than most businesswomen to overcome the stereotypes that surround her.
- They are afraid. They want to grow, and yet they fear growth. They worry about word processing and what it will do to them. They search for—and yet are wary of—work that will replace that taken over by machines. And they fear ending up in an automated secretarial pool.

This book was written to help the assistant deal with these conflicts and frustrations so she can become more worthwhile to herself and to her organization.

FOCUS OF THE BOOK

It was a difficult decision for me when I decided to gear this book toward women. I didn't want to relegate women to the "ghetto" of the assistant; nor did I want to ignore the reality that over 95 percent of all assistants are women. I decided to reflect the reality.

Unfortunately, many women assume that any material directed to them is remedial in nature and not the "real" stuff that men get. I can assure the reader that this book is not Mickey Mouse. Aside from the first chapter on women in business, the rest of the book would be useful to any male assistant or supervisor. And, in fact, much of the material is used in my other management seminars.

A GENERAL OUTLINE

This book consists of 11 chapters. Each one looks at a different area of concern to the assistant.

In Chapter 1 we explore the barriers that may be set up for the assistant because she is a woman. These impediments may be external or they may be internal, generated by the assistant herself.

Chapter 2 looks at the role of the assistant—what she does, how she should act, what she should avoid, and what she can expect. We also give some guidelines to determine the "fit" between the assistant and her organization.

Basic good human relations is the subject of Chapter 3. From individual differences we move on to explore a motivational model. There is also an explanation of an approach to better interpersonal relations in general.

In Chapter 4 the topic is the manager. A model is provided to show the assistant how well she matches up with her manager. An approach to changing mismatches is also discussed.

We look at time management in Chapter 5. I present the reader with a system for better time management for herself and her manager. Some timesaving tips for managers and assistants are included.

In Chapter 6 the topic is communication. We start by looking at the communication process itself and go on to give the reader tips on improving speaking, listening, and writing skills.

Chapter 7 builds on the previous chapter by explaining the uses of two specific communication models: assertiveness and active listening. There is a self-diagnosis scale to evaluate the reader's assertiveness and practice exercises in both techniques.

Solving problems and making decisions is the focus of Chapter 8. Examples are followed through to explain the approach to each. There is a section on the uses of creativity to enhance basic problem-solving techniques.

Chapter 9 looks at the assistant as a supervisor of other people. Guidelines are given in five areas of the supervisory aspects of the assistant's job: selection, orientation, training, delegation, and appraisal. Some "don't be" supervisors are described.

In Chapter 10 we explain an approach to career planning. Both long-range and short-term "next step" planning techniques are shown. We look at eight different routes to advancement for the assistant.

Chapter 11 is a selection of questions that assistants have asked me in seminars. It brings together the major kinds of concerns they seem to have.

HOW TO USE THE BOOK

I hope you will enjoy reading this book. I would also like to give you some hints on how you can best use it as a learning tool.

- Do the exercises in each chapter as you read. It's always tempting to skip over these parts in a book, but you will learn much more if you take time to do them.
- After reading each chapter, decide on one or two items you would like to apply in your own work situation. Set goals and decide how you will carry them out.
- Discuss what you read with other assistants. Talking about new ideas helps you to sift out what you can use. Then you will be more likely to apply them.
- Use the book as a reference when you have a particular problem. Reading the portion relevant to your difficulty may give you some ideas on how to deal with it.
- Do further reading in the subjects that most interest you. I've arranged the selected reading list by subject matter so that it will be easier for you to choose the best books for you.

In closing, I would like to thank the many assistants with whom I have worked in seminars and whose hopes and experiences are reflected in this book.

1

THE WOMAN IN BUSINESS

or "What's a nice girl like you doing in a place like this?"

Like most women in the business world, you have probably experienced problems that have to do with the fact that you are female. Such problems range from blatant discrimination aimed at keeping women from advancing to subtler types of treatment that make them feel unwanted or put down. Let us see if you identify with any of these assistants:

Sherry is a college-educated woman who holds a very responsible position as assistant to a vice-president in a large organization. She was recently given the opportunity to represent her boss at an industry association convention. While there, she attended the policy sessions and, a number of times, raised her hand to make a point. Each time she was politely listened to and the meeting went on with no other consideration of her idea. She feels the others at the meeting were making assumptions about her ideas because she is a woman.

Susan has been trying to get out of her assistant's job for two years. Everybody—her boss, the personnel department, her colleagues—tells her to be patient; the company will find a place for a competent person like her to move into management. She is beginning to feel that she is in a dead-end position, mainly because she is a woman.

Karen is an executive assistant to the personnel manager of a large company. She has been given a special assignment to compile a report on the state of employee absenteeism in the company. To get the information she needs for the report, she has scheduled appointments with various department heads. She has found it appallingly difficult to get the information she needs. She has been stalled, ignored, and dismissed by these managers. She feels that being a woman is a large part of the problem.

Barbara has recently been promoted from executive secretary to administrative assistant. Since her promotion she has noted a certain coolness on the part of the office staff. When she asks people to do something (supervisory duties are part of her new position) she hears remarks like people "forgetting who they are" and "throwing their weight around." She is beginning to feel very isolated in her success. What's wrong with being a successful woman?

What may be wrong in each of these cases is that too many people—including sometimes the woman herself—still do not expect a woman to be successful—a leader, powerful, in a responsible position.

THE SOURCE OF THE CONFLICT

As far as I am concerned, a woman in business today has to deal with two related, yet different, problems. She has to handle the possible negative attitudes of those around her and she has to handle her own doubts and guilt feelings.

Most women who have a business career have experienced at one time or another a conflict between that career and their womanhood. Sometimes the conflict is out in the open, a result of manipulative pressures on the part of other people who question whether woman and businessperson can exist in the same body. Other times it is a more covert, nagging questioning within the woman herself about who she is as a woman and what she should be. I strongly believe that any woman who wishes to be successful in the business world must look at the nature of this conflict in herself and work at resolving it. Otherwise this conflict will affect her, those around her, and her career.

A while ago, during a seminar for administrative assistants, I was discussing with the group the traditional role of women and how it might affect their ability to do a job in the business world. One of the registrants raised her hand and said: "That's the way I was born and that's how I am!" If you choose to accept the fact that you were born being what you are and behaving as you do, you will do very little to change that. If, however, you accept the idea that much of people's behavior, including yours, is learned rather than innate, the possibility of changing that behavior becomes apparent. Of course, you have the right to decide whether you want to.

To help you to understand the origins of "female" behavior, I'd like you to try a little exercise. On a sheet of paper draw a line lengthwise down the center. On the left, write the title "Girls are," and on the right, write the heading "Boys are." Now, without thinking too carefully about it, write down all the words you think of to describe boys and girls under each heading. Please do this before reading further.

There are no right and wrong answers on your list, but let's compare your ideas with some typical responses of women:

Girls are: sweet, innocent, gentle, trusting, shy, quiet, pretty, clean, emotional, nice, affectionate

Boys are: leaders, independent, forceful, aggressive, responsible, strong, commanding, opinionated, logical, stony-faced, loud

You probably used similar adjectives to reflect your innermost feelings on the "correctness" of male and female behaviors. Where does this notion of right behavior come from? A good deal of it is learned. From the time we are young, our society attempts to teach us what it considers appropriate behavior; much of that behavior is related to sex. It is almost as if a blueprint were used to create in us the right kind of behavior according to society's notions.

Listen in at an average playground, for example, and you will find grown-ups (with all good intentions) doing things like this: a mother telling a little girl not to dirty her pretty dress; a father demanding that his son stop crying because boys don't cry; a grandmother praising her grandson for climbing to the top of the jungle gym; a babysitter admonishing a little girl for fighting. In thousands of experiences like this when we are young, a great deal of our adult behavior is preprogrammed into us. And much of our adult life is spent acting out that early conditioning.

YOUR EXPERIENCE

To carry this concept further, take a few minutes to look inside yourself to identify your own learning experiences in some critical aspects of life. For each of the following ten words, write down what you learned as a young child about it. As you do this, remember that teaching can occur by actions as well as by words. For example, if you were told to stick up for your rights, but every time you did you were reprimanded for being so pushy, you learned *not* to stand up for your rights. Now try the exercise.

Marriage	Conflict
Ambition	Feminine behavior
Career	Success
Appearance	Problem solving
Mechanical things	Emotions

Again, your own answers will be individual to your life and experience, and can be neither right nor wrong. Here are some actual responses I've gotten from women:

Marriage—security, necessary, the objective, end of the line
Ambition—get along, marry, have children
Career—secretary, nurse, teacher, social worker
Appearance—sexy, pretty, clean
Mechanical things—impossible, for boys
Conflict—no-no, don't rock the boat
Feminine behavior—soft, weak, giving, delicate
Success—marriage, good cook
Problem solving—not necessary, they'll do it
Emotions—crying is okay, feel

WHAT HAPPENS ON THE JOB

Assuming that many, if not most, women have experienced these types of ideas in their childhood, how can such notions affect grown women? Let's look at a typical day in the life of a stereotyped North American socialized woman:

She arrives at her job as an executive secretary and the first thing she sees is that someone has left some dirty coffee cups on the desk next to hers. She quickly picks them up and takes them to the washroom to rinse them out because she can't stand the mess.

On her way back to her desk, a male manager acquaintance greets her and compliments her on her new dress. She feels very good at receiving this attention, but is not too happy about the pat on the derriere she also received.

Back at her desk, the phone rings and the person on the other end wants to speak to her manager. Although her boss has given her the responsibility of handling this type of problem, the caller on the other end insists that he must speak to the manager. She gives in to avoid a hassle.

Meanwhile two of her manager's subordinates have come to her within a half hour demanding a top priority on some material to be typed and collated. She agrees to both, although she can't possibly get both done. She doesn't know how to say no and still be nice.

As the day quiets down a bit, she drifts into her favorite daydream, in which she is the manager. She is hoping that somehow something will happen to bring that about. She would not say anything to her boss about her ambitions because that would be too forward.

At a staff meeting that afternoon, the new department project is discussed. She has a momentary urge to add something to the discussion but stops herself because her ideas probably aren't that important. And what would they think of her if she spoke up? At 4:30 her manager tells her she'll have to stay late to finish up a priority item. She wants to refuse, but she can't fight her boss. Tears come to her eyes as she momentarily clenches her fists. But she sighs and settles in for an evening's work that will take twice as long because she doesn't want to be there.

Exaggerated? Yes. Unreal? No. What you have just witnessed in this little vignette is a woman who would like to act differently but doesn't know how. More important, she doesn't think she can.

There are some things in life and in ourselves that we must learn to live with. One young woman manager I know experienced difficulty in life because she is very tall (six feet). At one point, she had even consulted a surgeon about having her legs shortened. The day she realized that her height was a virtually unchangeable fact of her life was the day her life changed. She not only accepted it but she started to use it. She found out that she can be imposing in a boardroom.

Most women are physically weaker than most men and cannot change that. But many other facets of so-called "femininity" *are* changeable. As long as women think they must be "nice" because it is in their genes, like long legs, they will remain that way. But if they see that a good deal of behavior is the result of instruction and find that behavior a barrier in life, they have taken the first step to change.

Let's review what we've established so far. You, like most women, have probably had some kind of learning experiences in your early life that taught you that to be feminine you had to be relatively gentle, soft-spoken, and nonopinionated. You, like most women, have probably had experiences in your adult life when you felt you weren't as effective as you could be in a situation and wondered if you could change that. You now see the relationship between the early learning and the present time. But how does this learning mechanism work?

MESSAGES

Our brains have the most fantastic storage area of any computer ever devised. Not only do we have all our experience stored somewhere in there, but we also have short-cut guidelines built in to give us ways to act in repetitive types of situations. A simple example of this is what happens automatically to most of us when we stop at a curb to cross a street. We get directions on how to do it.

Next time you are at a curb, stop and ask yourself what you are telling yourself to do. You will probably find you have in your head very useful guidelines you learned in childhood: "Cross at the Green, Not In Between" and "Stop, Look, and Listen" are examples of these. Some of you may even recall a jingle you learned in kindergarten or at home. Most of the time, when crossing the street, we're not even aware that the "message" is being sent; we just respond to it unconsciously by, for example, looking both ways before we cross the street.

In the same way, we all as adults respond unconsciously to many messages telling us how to behave in certain situations. The assistant in the story, for example, might have washed the coffee cups in response to an implanted message that said "Girls are neat." She may have been following orders that said "Don't stand out in a crowd" when she couldn't speak up at that meeting. And she cried at the thought of working overtime when she really wanted to be angry because nice girls don't get angry.

At this point in the chapter I feel it is necessary to stop and say a few words about the ideas I've been presenting. Many of you may be thinking one of the following:

1. All this about programming and messages in the head is nonsense or
2. It's true but you've been too hard on parents and society and/or
3. "They've" ruined me and I'd better get back at "them"!

To answer the first objection, let me point out that all the great writers on human psychology, from Freud on, have said, in one way or another, that each person is greatly influenced, if not formed, in early childhood. It's not whether this type of influencing—or what I call programming—exists, but what we do about it. "I am what I am" is a very self-limiting concept.

As for the second objection, I meant to say that most parents—and our society in general—have at all times in history done what they thought was best for their children. Tight corsets and back straighteners were inflicted on many nineteenth-century children. At the beginning of the twentieth century, education was not deemed to be necessary for the average child. Child-raising experts in the last 30 years have promoted permissiveness.

Each generation has been prepared for the future according to the values, resources, and even fads of the society at the time. In the last 20 years, though, our North American society has changed enormously. Who could have foreseen the intense mobility of the society, the high divorce rate, the technological advances? Accordingly, who could have prepared their children, and especially their "girl" children, for this world?

All parents raise their children for an unforeseen world. In the past, when life moved slowly, such "training" was more effective because each generation changed relatively little. But consider the fact that if you are now 50, you were raised for a depression world; if you are now 40, you were raised for a world at war; if you are 30, you were raised in the hue and cry of permissiveness; and if you are 20, you were raised on dissent! (See the book by Massey, which goes into this concept fully.)

Relating this question of childhood preparation to femaleness, many women who are now adults were raised for a world in which women were primarily homemakers. Parents, schools, churches, and the media all played their part in this preparation. (This isn't a matter of placing blame; it is an attempt to help you understand the cause of a great deal of your behavior.)

A third response to the ideas we've been looking at is to feel that if the formative influences in your life would do that to you, you have a right to be angry about it. Unfortunately, too many people think that women's seminars are primarily "bitch" sessions against men. Of course that's not true. In fact, men have lost out too in the traditional socialization process. A woman may be at a disadvantage because she learned to be dependent, but a man can be at a disadvantage because he has learned he must be the leader, can't be emotional, and has to be the family breadwinner.

Traditional socialization of both men and women has its negative side (it has a positive side that we'll get to, so hang on) but all we can do—and must do—as adults is to look at ourselves as resources to be developed. Development starts with where you are right now.

WHAT IS STANDING IN YOUR WAY?

Because all of us—both men and women—have been influenced by ideas of what femaleness is, the woman in business tends to experience two kinds of difficulties: difficulties arising from the actions of other people that tend to limit her, and difficulties that come from self-induced barriers to effectiveness.

To enable you to look at how real these problems are in business, jot down as many answers as you can to this question: "Why aren't more women in management?" Some typical responses I've collected from women are:

Men don't accept women in business
Traditional role
Lack of education
No ambition
Limited by organization
Women aren't leaders
Other women
Home responsibilities
Husband
Don't think they can do it
Scared

Inability to plan career
Lack of motivation
Stereotyped jobs
Resentment of others
Lack of confidence

Many reasons are possible, but the purpose of this analysis is not to make you feel the weight of all the barriers. Look at the list, and your list, and you will find two different kinds of reasons listed. Items like "men don't accept," "organization limitations," "husband," and "other women" point to barriers that are outside ourselves, to the way other people are acting. On the other hand, things like "lack of education," "being scared," "home responsibilities," and "inability to plan" are directly related to us, to things we can learn to do, and to actions we can take.

When we are responsible for the barriers to our effectiveness, the road to change is direct, though not necessarily easy. If I perceive, for example, that one of the barriers to my development is my relative lack of self-confidence, I can find ways to improve that poor self-image and work on improving it.

Incidentally, many women don't realize how often they act against their own self-interest. To paraphrase the famous comic strip character Pogo: "We have met the enemy and he is us." How can a woman who has learned to be trusting see the manipulative people she may encounter? If a woman has learned to be sweet, how can she discipline or fire a subordinate? If a woman has learned to be demure, how can she speak up at a staff meeting?

When others' behavior is the barrier to effectiveness, the cure is not so obvious. If your boss, your husband, or someone else is not acting the way you want, unless you invite him to read this book or some other event occurs to affect his behavior, he will tend to keep on acting the same way. The only form of control you have over other people's behavior is your own behavior. Let me repeat that: The only way to change other people is to change yourself. Take a simple example. If my manager calls me "Sweetie" constantly and I hate it *but* I don't say anything about it, I am helping the behavior to continue. I may wish that the other person would notice my dislike of his habit, but unless I take some more direct action, he will keep on acting the same way. How you change your behavior to induce other people and circumstances to be helpful to you is what this book is about.

Men are not "bad." Most men don't get up in the morning and plan how they're going to "get" women. Instead, a great deal of discrimination by men is almost a "knee jerk" type of reaction—a repetition of thousands of similar types of behavior they have acted out with women before.

Let's look at one common assumption and see how it may affect behavior: A women is primarily a bearer of children and caretaker of the home. That assumption leads to these actions:

A woman has too much to do at home so I can't expect her to do demanding work on the job.

A woman can't work late or travel and therefore I won't promote her.

A woman's opinion in business is not worthwhile and I will ignore it.

DEALING WITH ASSUMPTIONS

To overcome such assumptions (many of them deep-seated and unconscious) the woman in business must be prepared to deal with them. The best way to do that is to act in such a way that the assumption is seen as clearly untrue. Let's peek in on some administrative assistants who don't realize that their behavior may actually be perpetuating a negative position for themselves.

Janet is an efficient, attractive woman of about 50. She has been an assistant to this manager for the last five years. She prides herself on the fact that she doesn't consider herself too good to perform many services for her manager that some of the younger women won't. Each morning when he arrives, his tea, prepared just the way he likes it, is waiting for him. She does a lot of other things for him, too. He's rather young and inexperienced, after all, so she sees helping him as part of her job. She has done this with a number of managers during her career. Last year when he was taking those graduate courses, she did a lot of typing for him, sometimes working late hours. But he's always telling the other managers how helpful she is and how he couldn't get his work done without her.

Janet wonders how there would be time in the job of the assistant to do all those other things she's heard about at a seminar she attended: preparing reports, supervising the office staff, finding more efficient ways to carry out the work of the department. God knows she's busy enough just getting that man to where he's supposed to be and looking halfway decent!

Warning: Beware of a tendency to mother your boss. Mothers are helpful and nice to have around, but they never get paid back for what they do.

Terry is young enough to be Janet's daughter. She is also an administrative assistant and sees herself as one of the "new breed." You won't catch Terry playing maid to her manager, but then she is not above a little sexual manipulation to get what she wants. Terry knows just how to dress to get the attention of the men in the office. She'd never give up personal dictation, because her manager enjoys walking around while he dictates and occasionally peering down the front of her dress. She's been propositioned a number of times but she doesn't intend to bargain except for the best deal. If sex is an advantage women have in business, why not use it?

Warning: Sex objects are transitory playthings. Who would entrust the organization to a plaything?

Doris is a "new woman." She would consider it practically immoral to be either a mother or a sex object to her manager. She reads all the new books, belongs to some professional women's associations, and is working very hard at going from an assistant's role to that of a manager. Doris is determined not to become stereotyped. For that reason she is very aware of her behavior and makes sure she doesn't act too "female." At a meeting, she can outswear any man. Being accused of being aggressive is music to her ears, because it means she's outdoing men at their own game. She's made some enemies in the office with her "direct" approach, but Doris considers that part of the game. Hasn't she seen men act the same way?

Warning: A woman can't be a man. She can only be a more effective woman. The "imitation male" woman manager is a second-rate copy.

It's clear from these examples that Terry and Janet are self-destructing by placing themselves in a traditional and relatively powerless position. But what about Doris? Her ineffectiveness comes from a type of overcompensation. Blatant nonfemale behavior on the part of a woman in business tends to create bad feelings in both men and women—in women because Doris is so abrasive; in men because she is so "unfeminine."

It's not easy to be a woman in management. Her behavior is often scrutinized carefully to see if she will be allowed to "join the club." And we are all subjected to measurement against other people's ideas of what a woman should be.

THE OTHER SIDE

A great deal of this chapter has been spent looking at the problems of being a woman in business. It is time to look at the other side. We definitely have pluses to bring to the business world *because* we are women, not in spite of that fact. I would like to talk about some of these advantages.

Sensitivity

Traditionally women have been considered to be people oriented and men thing oriented. In the business world this quality in women was seen as a fault—an excessive softness that would interfere with effectiveness. However, the workforce has changed enormously in the last 20 years. Expectations are higher. There are many competing demands for a person's interest. Most important, a person does not have to work to live. Because of these widespread changes, most employees today demand leadership that is sensitive to their needs. A woman manager's willingness and propensity to be sensitive to other people can therefore be seen as an important managerial skill.

Mediating Ability

Earlier in the chapter we looked at common "messages" that women carry with them. Often they have a set that has to do with not fighting: "Nice girls don't fight"; "Don't rock the boat"; "Be nice"; "See all sides." Like many of the other traditionally female behaviors, this can be seen as negative or positive. The woman who never has an opinion and never stands up for her own opinion is ineffective. But the capacity to approach a conflict from an objective standpoint and the desire to let everybody win are definite pluses in today's business world. The power play approach, though necessary at times, has increasing limitations, and a woman can sometimes win more by letting both sides win.

Listening Ability

Not all women are necessarily better listeners than men. However, some of our common life experiences have given women an edge in this important communication skill. Look at a group of people at any cocktail party. In most cases, a man will be talking and a woman will be nodding her head. Listening attentively to a man is a social skill many women have been taught. (Instruction for your first date: Just ask him what sport he plays and then listen.)

Some of you are probably ready to lynch me at this point, protesting that this kind of behavior is exactly the subservient type of activity from which women have to escape. Yet one of the most important management skills in today's world is listening. This skill is necessary to motivate, to counsel, to manage. Of course, listening must be balanced with a willingness to assert one's own ideas. Still, listening itself is a vital management skill in organizations, and many women have already learned that skill.

Intuition

One of the beauties of our present-day world is that many of the things that used to be considered strange are now being seen in a new light. "Women's intuition" used to be a focus of great amusement. The so-called sixth sense was sometimes laughingly ascribed to women as part of their peculiarity. Then the psychologists started to study this phenomenon and came up with the interesting thought that intuition is often unconscious observation. In that way, intuition can be seen as a conscious recognition of many unconsciously received signals.

When a woman comes away from a social gathering, for example, and says to her husband: "There's something about that man we met I just don't like," she may be saying, in effect, "I received a great many clues from his tone of voice, posture, use of hands, way of speaking, and so on, that mean something different from his words.

Some people are very intuitive, and this sense gives them valid information; others are misled when they try to use this faculty. Women tend to have developed intuition more (because of their child-bearing role?), and if you are one of the women who gets good information this way, use it. I'm not suggesting that you run your life by "feelings." I'm suggesting that you monitor your own intuitive responses. If they turn out to be valid, rely on them. If your intuition is unreliable, forget it.

Incidentally, intuition is an excellent example of what sometimes happens when one group of people finds that another group of people has a good thing going for it. As soon as the psychologists began to clarify the nature of intuition, it became more accepted in organizations as a source of information. Now those darling males have completely taken over the concept. When you hear a male manager make reference to the fact that he has a "gut feeling" about something, realize that he is using an updated and masculinized version of our woman's intuition.

Whole-Person Approach

Women who work usually have two jobs—one at "work" and one at home. Women have always had to balance many aspects of life; if a woman got a job it was always in addition to, not instead of, her job at home. That sense of work fitting into a total life pattern is a positive one we can bring to the organization.

Women are more efficient as managers because they can't afford the luxury of bringing work home; they always have work waiting at home for them. Women managers may have more of an awareness, too, of employees' needs outside the job because they experience the pressure of these needs themselves.

In this first chapter, my aim has been to show you how your femaleness can affect the rest of your job. Both you and those around you make certain assumptions about you just because you are a woman. When these assumptions become barriers—either by the action of others or within your own mind—they must be dealt with. As we go through many skills in this book and you try them out, you may see these barriers come into play. Don't see them as permanent and unchanging. Rather, learn to handle them as you set out to improve your effectiveness in the role of the assistant.

2

THE ROLE OF THE ASSISTANT

or "What do I do now?"

In this chapter we're going to look at what the assistant does. All the other chapters have to do with the skills you need to carry out that role. Some women in assistant roles have the title of administrative assistant but are performing little more than a clerical role. Others may have the title of secretary but the responsibilities of an assistant. Such common occurrences make the definition of the role rather difficult. But it is possible to distinguish, at least, between various levels of performing as an assistant. Once you know where you are, in relation to these levels, you can work to make your job the position you want it to be.

In general, organizations have a progression in the role of the assistant through these job titles: secretary, executive secretary, administrative assistant. As I use the terms, an assistant could conceivably move from one level to the next while reporting to the same manager, depending on the content of her job. Let's look at some characteristics of each of these positions.

Secretary

1. Acts under direct supervision of boss.
2. Has minimum amount of personal responsibility.
3. Is competent in, and uses, clerical skills such as typing and filing.

Executive Secretary

1. Usually works for a top executive.
2. Needs less supervision from manager; shows more initiative.
3. Often has special responsibilities delegated from manager.
4. Usually has more experience.
5. Has more authority to get things done.
6. Has major responsibility to organize manager.

Administrative Assistant

1. Does minimal secretarial work, if any; may have a secretary.
2. Is responsible for specific delegated duties such as reports, research, special projects.
3. May act in manager's absence.
4. Receives minimal, if any, direct supervision from manager.
5. Makes decisions on own.
6. Usually selects, supervises, appraises office staff.
7. May represent manager at off-site functions.
8. May be responsible for preparation and follow-up of budget.

How can you use these guidelines? If you are not already an administrative assistant, they give you some idea of what the position entails. You can work toward taking on those functions. If you feel you are already performing the duties of an assistant but do not have the title, you have a number of possible actions, depending on your situation.

First of all, you should clarify your job with your manager. Then be prepared to persist in getting the title to reflect the work you are already doing. Remember, though, that in some companies the title of administrative assistant doesn't exist. When that is the case, you are either going to have to be content with the job and its rewards without a title—or seek out another company where you can get a title.

Some administrative assistants have a title but find that their work doesn't match that title. Such assistants are often demotivated in their jobs because they do not have the work they would like. These people, too, have to look into the relative possibilities of convincing the manager to change the situation—that is, increase their responsibilities—or look elsewhere for more challenge.

DEFINING THE ASSISTANT

We're going to look at the job of the assistant, not with a textbook definition, but on the basis of the real experience of assistants surveyed in seminars. We're going to see what the job is made of, what personal characteristics are necessary to carry it out, and what the chief mistakes to avoid are.

An assistant is exactly that, and because of it, the nature of her job is different from most others in the organization. The responsibilities of the assistant arise out of the responsibilities of another person—her manager—and her chief function is to assist that person in getting his or her work done. Let's look at the major parts of the assistant's job.

Organization

It could almost be said that this is the whole job of the assistant. It is certainly her chief responsibility—to organize the functions of the manager she works for.

This aspect of the job includes maintaining the executive's appointment calendar, making the best use of her and her manager's time, maintaining files for ready access, and systematizing procedures for efficient operations of the office. In practice, this part of the job may involve duties as diverse as devising a new filing system or writing a procedures manual to maintaining a tickler file or keeping a record of most commonly used telephone numbers.

Delegation

Everyone in management must know how to delegate. For the administrative assistant this may be harder, because she may not have full authority to supervise the staff members to whom she is delegating.

There is a science—and an art—to getting others to do what you want them to do. It starts with clarifying in your own head what you want, and then moves to communication with the other. In addition, effective delegation includes motivation and appraisal. To delegate effectively, the assistant must avoid seeing herself as either a martyr ("I'd better do it myself instead of delegating it") or a dictator ("Now *I'm* the boss").

Coordination/Communication Between People and Departments

Whether the assistant is completely responsible for a project or is doing one small part of it, she often needs to work with many other people to get it done. Most of the time there is no clear line of authority between the assistant and these others. That means that her effectiveness depends on her own interpersonal skills.

Written Communication

The administrative assistant is often responsible for a great deal of written communication. She may have to compose minutes, prepare reports, write letters, or even write presentations for her boss. She needs the ability to put her words down in a clear, concise manner. She must also realize that written communication has a disadvantage that spoken communication does not; the writer is not there to ensure that the receiver will read it. Motivation must be built into the writing.

Public Relations

The assistant is often the first—and sometimes the only—person with whom a caller or visitor comes in contact. Her behavior will be seen as representative of her manager. By her actions she can either create good relations with other departments and thus facilitate working with them—or set up barriers.

MOST IMPORTANT CHARACTERISTICS

Now that we have looked at the most important parts of an assistant's job, let's get some idea of the traits and characteristics you need to be an effective assistant.

Informed

Part of the job of the assistant is to foresee possible problems and take action before they occur. She may also have to act during the manager's absence. She cannot do these things unless she keeps her eyes and ears open. The assistant has the responsibility of keeping up with what is going on in the company and the department. She should know what the goals of the company are. She should educate her manager to keep her informed on the happenings. She should read all material that crosses her desk, and she should be alert to what is new, whether it is a new piece of equipment or a new person.

Reliable

To reach her own job objectives as well as to serve as an example, the administrative assistant must be reliable. This extends from such basics as being on time to a general results-oriented approach. A good part of the assistant's credibility is related to her ability to get the job done.

Diplomatic

The assistant normally has very little muscle. Without that kind of raw power, she has to rely on her personal influence to be effective. Whether they are customers, clerks, other managers, or members of the board of directors, she must be mindful of others' feelings when she deals with them.

Forward-looking/Flexible

Creativity is "in" in organizations today. That doesn't mean that managers are turning into artists. It does mean that effective managers realize that many problems are not going to be solved by simple, time-worn solutions. The assistant, too, has to have an attitude that allows for an openness and acceptance of new ideas.

"Why do we have to do it this way?" from a new junior person may be seen as either an act of defiance or the start of an inquiry that can lead to a better way of doing something. Most effective assistants I know have such an approach to their whole job. Whether they recommend a color-coded filing system, a department call-board, a word processing system, or a "department employee of the month," these assistants are open to new ways of getting results.

Dedicated/Committed

By this guideline I do not mean blind loyalty; I mean involvement. To be effective, the administrative assistant must like her job, do it well, get rewarded for it, and see herself as growing in it. These are the elements of a motivated commitment to the job.

Up to now, in this chapter, we have been looking primarily at what you must do or be in order to be an effective administrative assistant. But in addition, to help yourself achieve such competence, you must be sure you are getting what you want from the job. Although it is not usually written, a contract exists between all employees and the organization for which they work. The company receives the time, effort, and abilities of the employees. The employees earn money and other rewards.

To be an effective, committed assistant, you must be clear on what you want out of your job and be willing to make it happen. Let's look at what an informal survey of assistants came up with in terms of job expectations. (This might be a good part of the book to share with your manager!)

EXPECTATIONS

Recognition

The assistant wants to have her efforts appreciated. She's not talking about flowers or even flowery words. She wants an honest "thank you" for the effort she puts into her job.

Responsibility

Unfortunately, many assistants have the title but not the real job. Because of this, they feel they are glorified "go-fers." All management literature today says that people need responsibility to be motivated on their jobs, and the assistant is no different. She provides an enormous service to her manager by taking on responsibilities he or she might otherwise have to handle.

Cooperation

The administrative assistant needs to be part of the manager's world. She needs to be informed in order to be effective. She needs to have things explained in order to be committed. And she must feel that there is an atmosphere of two-way communication—not just listening and responding to what her manager says, but also having a manager who is open to her ideas and suggestions.

Respect

The assistant needs the respect that is due her as a human being and as a professional. Whether the manager shows this respect by calling her by name or by giving her some latitude in the methods she uses, she wants to know she is considered worthy of the kind of treatment that makes her feel important and valued. She doesn't want to be referred to as "my girl" or to have to work overtime because of management's mistakes.

Authority

There is a terrible sin in management referred to as "responsibility without authority." It means that you've been given something to do but not the power to do it. Impossible situation? Absolutely. Yet many assistants are in exactly that position. When the assistant has a responsibility delegated to her, she must be given the authority by her manager to do it. A simple written memo to the office, for example, informing people that the manager's assistant is now in charge of arranging vacation schedules will give her the authority she needs to do the job. Otherwise she may be seen as someone trying to take over for her own aims. When that happens, people may resist cooperating with her.

Trust

The assistant doesn't want to receive responsibility and authority and then have her manager hang over her to see if she can really perform. One of the important aspects of delegation is knowing how much control to use. In general, with regard to this expectation, assistants are saying that their managers retain too much control. Less control has its risks, but the payoff is an assistant who is both competent and committed.

Opportunity

How far an assistant wants to go in her career is an individual matter, but no one wants to be labeled as incapable of going any further. Within the boundaries of their own career choice, assistants want the chance to grow. That could mean a new responsibility, an invitation to attend a training seminar, on-the-job instruction on a new piece of equipment, or help in becoming a manager herself.

Money

Most top executives agree that a competent assistant can make an enormous difference in their ability to get things done. Such ability should not come cheap.

THE DON'TS

We've been taking an approach to studying the role of the assistant that is based on a navigational technique called "triangulation." Essentially, it consists in focusing on one point from three different directions in order to pinpoint a position. So far, we have focused in on the role of the administrative assistant from the vantage points of most important parts of the job, important characteristics, and expectations. Now we're going to make another approach—the chief "no-no's." Every job has certain key points about which, if the novice is lucky, she is told and warned. Here are some of my tips on what to beware of in the job of the administrative assistant.

Don't Become a Dragon Lady

Some assistants learn that they can wield an enormous amount of power by controlling entry to their manager's office. Screening visitors is a valid and important part of the assistant's job, but shielding the manager too much can end up with his being kept ignorant of something he needed to know. That will backfire on you. The watchdog attitude also creates a lot of bad feelings. Sometimes you have to say no to people, but let them feel you'd like to say yes.

Don't Throw Your Weight Around

Especially with "pounds" you don't have. Be careful about assuming responsibility you haven't been given and using it to your own ends. Everyone wants to have influence over others, but if you lead others to think you have more than you do, it will backfire when your manager finds out. He won't like it.

Don't Intimidate Subordinates

Some people wait until they are the "boss" and then treat their subordinates just the way every bad boss they've ever had treated them. Because you are boss doesn't mean you have complete control. Be aware that you can't force people to be committed, motivated, or loyal. Those kinds of results come from leading people, not pushing them.

Don't Be Perfect

Perfection is not only uncomfortable for others; it is almost impossible for you. A need to be perfect leads to a tendency to cover up one's mistakes and to develop an overbearing attitude with others. The assistant who has her nose in the air may end up tripping over her own feet.

Don't Be a "Yes-Man"

We women have sometimes been accused of imperfectly imitating men in the organization. This is one kind of man you don't want to imitate. If your relationship with your manager is confined to following orders, you are doing both of you a disservice—a disservice to yourself because you will eventually resent your inability to express your own ideas and a disservice to your manager because he will be deprived of a truly effective assistant.

TUNING IN TO YOUR ORGANIZATION

Every organization has a personality. It has age, sex, virtues, vices, and even quirks. What your organization is like affects you in your job. It can determine what you can do, how you have to do it, and how far you can go. The more you see yourself as an important part of that organization and see where you fit in, the more motivated you will be. So let's look at your organization.

Take a sheet of paper and across the top write "My Organization." Now make three horizontal headings: (1) Company Purpose, (2) Where I Fit In, and (3) Company Personality. Under purpose I'd like you to write why your company exists—and I don't mean to make money, I mean what it offers in the way of a product or service to its customers. Your company's purpose may be written somewhere in the company literature, or you can just put it in your own words, such as "to manufacture, sell, and service specialized electronic equipment," or "to provide social services to the community," or "to mine and sell coal."

Under the second column, I'd like you to write down the way you personally help your company to achieve its purpose. You may assist a plant manager, for example, and in your position you are contributing toward the manufacture of the product. Or you may assist a personnel vice-president and be instrumental in supplying the labor necessary to produce the organization's product. You may assist a data processing manager and thereby contribute to reporting systems that enable the company to be more effective. In all honesty, this part of the exercise is designed to overcome the "just a secretary" syndrome.

The surer you are of your contribution to the company, the more motivated you will be.

In the third column, I want you to try a very useful exercise that will also be fun. Imagine that your company is a person or a thing. Who or what would it be? Think for a minute and then write it down. Your company is the environment for your accomplishment, satisfaction, and growth in your job. You have to tune in to that environment to be able to link your goals with those of the organization. Here are examples from working assistants:

> My company is new and fast-moving. If I were to describe it, I'd say it's a red sports car. What that means to me is a lot of pressure in my job because things are moving so fast. But it also means an attitude of acceptance toward new ideas. They're not bogged down in the past, because they don't have any. That gives me a chance to be innovative. It means opportunity for me to grow with the company. It's also very exciting!

> My company is Queen Victoria. We're a big public utility with lots of money and lots of rules. You know, you get the feeling that there's a way to do it and a way not to do it with everything, and you'd better do it their way if you want to get along. They're very conservative and cautious about most things. I'm pretty content, though, because the pace is just about right for me. I'm the kind of person who wants to do her job and do it well, but that's about it. I get my regular increases and have a good working environment, and the company sponsors lots of activities for employees. I guess you could say the "queen" takes good care of her subjects.

> I work for a company that's like a chicken running around with its head cut off. We're a community agency that's built on lots of good purpose, but sometimes that purpose gets lost with everybody's pet ideas and projects. We have to be very responsive to the government, too, because we get a lot of our funding there. And that means red tape and paperwork. Sometimes I get so harried I feel like standing up in the middle of everyone scurrying around and yelling 'Where are we going?' We're supposed to have a management team come in this year to give some help in planning. I hope it can get everyone on the same track. Otherwise I'm going to look around for another position. I mean if you don't know where you're going, how do you ever get anything done? And that's just not satisfying enough for me.

Your own example will be unique, of course. Here are some guidelines to help you frame your characterization.

What is the pace of the organization or your department within that organization? Does that pace suit you?

What is your company's attitude toward innovation? Is it too dynamic—or too staid—to suit you?

What is your company's attitude toward women? What is the highest position a woman holds?

Is your company "male" (things) or "female" (people), and how does that affect your environment?

How old is your company? Is it a vigorous youngster, a declining old person, or a middle-aged person in the process of renewal?

How does your company reward its employees? Do the rewards fit your expectations?

What does your company see as success? Does it give its "goodies" to those who work hard, who play politics, or who show loyalty? How comfortable are you with that?

Notice that in each question you are asked to assess your compatibility with a certain aspect of the organization. That is the whole key to using your knowledge of your company. A good "fit" between you and your organization means that you have all the odds in your favor to be an effective member of the organization.

We have looked at what the job of the administrative assistant is in a variety of ways. In your own situation the most important way of attaining a concerted effort between you and your manager is to clarify your job with your manager. If you and your manager sit down to discuss your responsibilities, you may be surprised to find that you don't agree on them. That is true of many supervisor–subordinate relationships. Each assumes that both agree on what the job of the subordinate is.

A discussion could be an excellent way to get rid of routine things that could be done better by someone else and perhaps to take on additional, more challenging, responsibilities. Start thinking about you and your company as partners in an exchange. Is each of you satisfied with your part of the bargain? If not, how can that be rectified?

In this chapter, you have taken a good first step to defining your job. You have also begun to look at your job as a matter of choice. People who "find" themselves in jobs rarely make successes of themselves. To be effective you have to want to be there.

3

HOW TO WORK WELL WITH OTHERS

or "Why can't everyone be just like me?"

How well, or how poorly, you work with other people in your organization can make an enormous difference to you, not only in how effective you are, but also in how pleasant your work environment is. Pity the poor assistant who works in an environment in which gossip, petty rivalry, and an argumentative climate pervade the working day. Of course, the assistant's relationship with her boss is the biggest determinant of the work atmosphere; I've devoted all of Chapter 4 to that. The people environment I'm talking about here consists of the other people you encounter every day—other assistants, junior clerks, peers and subordinates of your manager, and people outside the organization.

How important are these in your work? If you have ever been stymied by your inability to get information from another person; if you have ever lived through a "personality conflict" with a co-worker; if you have ever left a job you loved because of one person, you know the answer to that question.

LEVELS OF INTERACTION

Like any other management-level person in the organization, an assistant must work well with at least three groups of people to be effective. In diagrammatical form, the place of a typical administrative assistant looks something like Figure 1. Relationship 1 is dealt with primarily in Chapter 4. Here we'll be dealing with ways to be more effective in areas 2, 3, and 4.

PEOPLE ARE DIFFERENT

Our society is full of sayings that attempt to make some kind of sense out of the subject of human behavior: "It takes all kinds to make a world." "Each to his own taste." "One man's meat is another man's poison." "Different strokes for different folks." What these maxims say is a major precept of human behavior: People are different.

To illustrate this, let's try a little experiment. Choose in your mind one person with whom you work. Now take a sheet of paper and draw a line lengthwise down the center. On the left-hand side, list eight to ten things you share in common with that person. On the right-hand side, list eight to ten ways in which you are different from that person. Your list will probably look something like:

Ways I am the same: We	*Ways I am different: I*
1. are female	1. wear glasses
2. like spicy food	2. am younger
3. enjoy coffee	3. spend more for clothes
4. vote liberal	4. ski
5. enjoy dancing	5. like Chinese food
6. grew up in the city	6. prefer detail work
7. like plants	7. hate the color purple
8. are shorter than average	8. have children
9. etc.	9. etc.

As long as the two of you are dealing in the area in which you share common attitudes and ideas, you will tend to understand and agree with each other. You can discuss, for example, the problems of being a woman in a business world that is traditionally male and be able to empathize with each other. You can share ideas on keeping house plants healthy. You can even appreciate the other's wanting to "take ten" and get a cup of coffee because you enjoy that kind of break, too.

But look at the right-hand side of the page. Imagine how easy it would be to get into conflict with this person over relatively small things. Her small handwriting bugs you when you forget your

Figure 1: Relationship of administrative assistant to others.

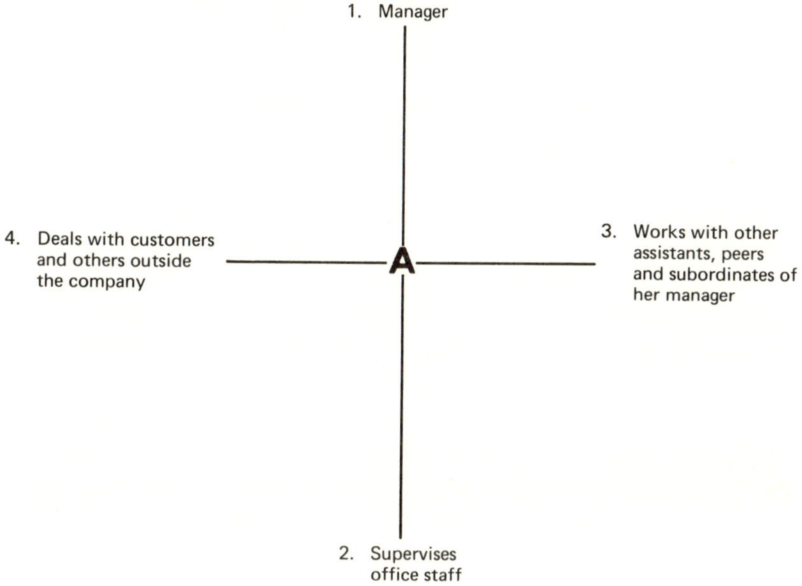

glasses. Your expensive clothes may cause her to feel jealous. And if you ever decide to invite her to lunch to improve relations between you, please don't take her to a Chinese restaurant.

The point of this little exercise is that a great deal of the conflict between people in offices—and elsewhere—stems from the differences between them. Each of us tends to assume that the *other person* should make an effort to appreciate *our* differences. (Why can't she write larger? She knows I forgot my glasses today.)

How different we are from each other. It's a wonder people get along at all. But don't give up. Recognizing a problem is the first step to solving it, and you've just taken that first step. Now you realize the importance of not assuming that everyone is like you, thinks like you, does things in the same way, or even wants what you want out of life.

A MODEL FOR MOTIVATION

A number of years ago, a prominent psychologist named Abraham Maslow created a model that you will find especially useful in dealing with those you supervise in the office. This model categorizes people according to their needs and is called the hierarchy of needs. It has five levels, starting with physiological needs, and going through security needs, belongingness needs, ego needs, and self-actualization needs.

According to Maslow's model, all human beings have essentially these same needs, although not necessarily all needs at the same time or in the same degree. To understand how needs affect people's behavior, think of a hungry person. She is "motivated" to walk to the refrigerator because her stomach *needs* food. Just so a lonely person is "motivated" to seek out people because she *needs* companionship.

Let's look more closely at what this model tells us and how it can be used by the assistant to motivate others. As we said, the first level in the model centers around physiological needs, the needs we have to satisfy to stay alive: air, water, food, warmth, and so on. According to Maslow, once a need is satisfied, it is no longer motivating. Although hunger may cause you to seek food, you know that after a meal you won't move to get more food. In the same way, once a person's physiological needs are satisfied, that person begins to think in terms of other needs.

Wouldn't it be nice, for example, to know that I won't ever go hungry again? This is an example of a security need. I might then be motivated to stock up with food to give me that security. Other security needs have to do with bodily safety and emotional security.

If the security needs are satisfied, a person starts to operate from belongingness needs, the need to be with people, to be liked, to be part of a group. We enjoy sharing a meal with others, for example, as a way of satisfying this need. Once a person has "enough" belongingness (and enough is individual for each of these levels) a person becomes interested in and motivated by what Maslow called esteem or ego needs.

There are two aspects to this level of needs: a person's self-esteem; that is, how she feels about herself; and feedback from the environment; that is, recognition from others. A person may give elegant dinner parties as a way of receiving recognition from her friends and thus satisfying esteem needs.

That last need level, once all the others are satisfied, is what Maslow called self-actualization needs. This is the need to be whatever you can be, to realize your potential. At this point, one might ask oneself whether it is worth putting all that energy into food and, instead, take up the guitar.

The hierarchy of needs operates commonly in organizational motivation. All organizations attempt to motivate those who work for them by giving them the opportunity to satisfy as many of their needs as possible on the job. You receive a paycheck that provides for basic physiological needs. You may have a pension plan, dental insurance, and job seniority to satisfy your security needs. Many companies, perhaps including yours, sponsor bowling teams, Christmas parties, and employee picnics to increase belongingness satisfaction. Titles, promotions, raises, and even a verbal pat on the back from your manager can satisfy your esteem needs. And in the interest of your long-term growth and self-actualization you may be encouraged to take on new responsibility from your manager or attend special seminars.

If your company provides for all the needs detailed in the hierarchy of needs, why is it important for you to know about this model? Because you as an individual supervisor can use the concept to increase the motivation of the people around you and create the kind of working relationships that will allow you and them to do the best work.

USING THE MODEL

The first way you can use Maslow's model to motivate those around you is to be aware that people have different needs and to respond to them accordingly. All of us are really operating from most of the needs at the same time. But many people seem to have one or two primary needs.

There is the older person, for example, who has worked in the same job for 25 years. She likes her job, doesn't want to go any higher, and loves the routine of it. She is attuned to security needs. To work with or supervise this worker, you should use the following approach:

Respect her for what she knows and learn from her.
Listen, sometimes, to how she feels about the "old days."
Introduce any changes to her gradually, with a great deal of support and allaying of fears.
Let her know what's going on so she won't think the worst.

On the other hand, take your young, just-out-of-high-school clerk. Her paycheck buys her clothes and fun, and she may see work only as a means to that end. Realize that she's attuned to a fast-paced view of life and is very much belongingness and esteem oriented. Approach her with these techniques:

Provide special fun rewards for excellent work.
Help her fit into the work group so her social needs are satisfied on the job.
Give her some different assignments once in a while to break the monotony.
Keep an ear open to her ideas.

Before going any further, I'd like to say a few words about the type of generalizing we're doing here. It is always easy, often useful, and sometimes dangerous. People are very complex. I have known people in their twenties who were primarily attuned to security needs and a 65-year-old who was working on her self-actualization needs by learning to ski. Models such as Maslow's must be applied to the individual carefully. Where does the person fit with the model, and where doesn't the person fit?

A second way you can use the hierarchy of needs is to make sure you provide those whom you supervise with the opportunity to satisfy as many needs as possible. It is only when people are satisfying their needs on the job that they are willing to give their best. Here are some questions you can ask yourself to see if you're getting the best out of your people:

Physiological Needs

1. Does your company pay a decent, competitive wage to its employees? If not, the cost in turnover and poor work may motivate *you* to convince higher management that changes are necessary.

2. Are enough rest breaks given to people during the day?

Security Needs

1. Do you give people the security of a job description so that they feel part of the company?

2. Do you have a few necessary rules that apply to everyone and are enforced fairly?

3. Are working conditions completely safe?

Belongingness Needs

1. Do you always introduce a new person to others in the office in positive terms so the rest of the group will want to accept her?

2. Do you help the people who aren't readily accepted by emphasizing their good points and bringing them in on things?

3. Do you bring your people together for group problem solving in areas of concern to them?

4. Do you act as a consultant and teacher to help others learn to get along with each other?

Esteem Needs

1. Do you fight that "cog in a wheel" feeling by showing each person how her work fits into the department?

2. Do you take time to show people what happens with the work that leaves their desk so they understand its importance—and their own?

3. Do you let higher management know when someone does an especially good job?

4. Do you use verbal praise, written memos, occasional lunches, and even small gifts to let people know how much you appreciate what they've done?

Self-Actualization Needs

1. Do you provide those who want it with the opportunity to learn new skills?

2. Do you encourage people to take advantage of company-sponsored courses and seminars?

3. Do you keep yourself open to new ideas for improvement in work methods that come from your people?

4. Do you set high but attainable standards of work to encourage people to grow and develop?

The more of these questions you can answer with a yes, the more likely you are to be doing all you can to bring out the best in your people.

USING YOUR AUTHORITY

We've looked at an approach to improving relationship 2, that between the administrative assistant and the people she supervises. Now let's concentrate on relationships 3 and 4. These interactions (between the assistant and peers, other managers, and people outside) are often the most difficult because the assistant is required to use a combination of personal skills and organizational clout to be effective. What we are talking about, specifically, is the question of authority.

You have two kinds of authority at your disposal to do your job: legitimate and personal. And you need both to get the job done, especially with peers and people outside your department or your company. Let's look at two administrative assistants who didn't understand this concept. The first Geraldine went to one of the managers of another department to get some confidential material for a report she had been asked to compile. Let's listen in on the conversation:

Geraldine: Mr. Jones, I'm Geraldine James, assistant to George King. I'd like to get the file on the XYZ Project for a report we're compiling. Is this a convenient time for you?

John: It's convenient, Miss James, but I can't let this file out of the department. Sorry.

Geraldine: We do need this file, Mr. Jones, and I can assure you nothing will happen to it.

John: Miss James, you look like a very honest person to me but I can't just give a file to anyone who walks in here and asks for one.

Geraldine: Mr. Jones, I understand your concern. And I do need that file. I'd be happy to sign a receipt for the material.

John: I'm afraid that won't help. I'll need George King's written authorization and then I can let you have the file.

Geraldine: Well, I guess I'll have to go back and get it. I'll see you, Mr. Jones, in a little while. And thank you.

What happened here? Geraldine used her personal authority. She spoke clearly. She established her own position. She showed empathy for John Jones's problem. She persisted with her own needs. All behaviors of a person exhibiting personal authority. But the formal authority that the organization demanded was missing.

Let's eavesdrop on another conversation to see what happens when formal authority is given but the personal authority is missing:

Geraldine: Hi, Mr. Jones, could I have the XYZ file?

John: You seem to know me, miss, but I don't know you.

Geraldine: Oh, yeah, well I'm Mr. King's secretary and he sent me to get the XYZ file.

John: Oh, he did, did he? Doesn't he know we need a formal request for that, Miss . . . Miss?

Geraldine: Gerry, my name is Gerry. And I have the request here. I think he's in a rush.

John: He's in a rush. Well, so are we. Leave it here and I'll get to it when I can.

Geraldine: Oh, okay.

Notice how Geraldine, in this case, made poor use of the formal authority she had. She did not communicate so as to promote respect for herself. She implied that John Jones had to give her the file. And she probably ended up going back to her boss and telling him that John Jones was being uncooperative, thereby creating bad relations between the two departments—as well as not getting the needed file. We'll look at some specific techniques in Chapter 7 to help you establish your personal authority. Remember, when you have been asked to do a job, get the authority from your boss that you need—a memo, a written request, a new job description—and add to its effectiveness with your communication techniques.

Now we're going to look at an approach that you will find useful on all levels of the organization.

THE U–I APPROACH TO BETTER RELATIONSHIPS

Getting along with other people is dependent on striking a balance between two different types of behavior: behavior that establishes respect for you as a person and behavior that recognizes the needs of others. Think, for a moment, of a person whom you respect and like and whom you consider to be a person with whom others "get along." Let's analyze her behavior to see if we can find out what makes her so effective. Ask yourself these questions about that person:

Is she in the habit of expressing her own ideas?
Is she a good listener?
Does she make you feel good when you're with her because she shows an interest in your life?
Is she competent in her job and decisive when necessary?
Is she willing to help out when necessary, and also to ask for help when she needs it?

If your answers are mainly yes, you have a model who is using the U–I approach to interpersonal relationships.

Whenever one person encounters another, each of them is thinking, in one way or another, exactly the same thing—I want. That's normal and necessary. Some people seem unable to express their wants, however. If you know someone like that, think how little respect you have for her—she's a doormat, a martyr, a marshmallow. On the other hand, if a person thinks *only* of what she wants, she becomes pushy. Using the U–I approach means balancing your own needs with those of others.

In any given situation you have four choices of action in terms of the U–I approach. The graph in Figure 2 explains those choices. Starting in the upper right-hand corner with Tessie the Tank, she puts her needs forward but ignores the other person's; she runs the other person down. Coming down to the lower right-hand corner, we meet the person who is unaware of anybody's needs; Corinne's just out of it. In the lower left-hand corner we see the typical traditional female; she's one for all and nobody for her. Marion ends up being stepped on. Wilma the Winner handles both sides and ends up . . . winning. (So do those who deal with her.)

It is the balancing of needs that makes the U–I approach so effective. Let us see how this concept works in practice and look at some specific ways you can improve your use of it.

THE U–I APPROACH IN ACTION

The situation is a familiar one. Helen Atkins, executive secretary to Harry Chambers, wants a raise. She enters his office.

Helen: Harry, do you have 15 minutes? I have something important I'd like to talk to you about.

Harry: Sure, Helen, it must be important for you to have such a serious look on your face. Sit down.

Helen: Harry, I think I deserve a raise.

Harry: Oh no, Helen, not you too! Everybody in this department thinks the same thing.

Helen: Yes, it must be hard for you making decisions on how to divide up the budget. But I'd like you to hear me out. As you know, Harry, in the last six months, I've taken over the billing of more client accounts as well as designing that new report form that is keeping us on track in the voucher area. That has given you more time, you've said yourself, to put in on the new automated system.

Figure 2: Types of administrative assistants.

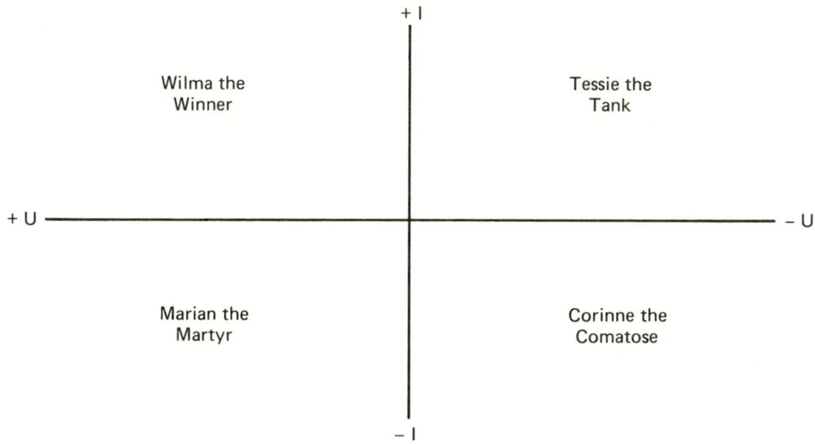

Harry: You *have* taken over a lot, Helen, and you've been doing it well. But there's only so much money in the budget. . . .

Helen: I understand you have limitations, Harry. But I'm not thinking just in terms of past reward. If I'm compensated as I think I deserve, I'd be able to increase my worth to you. For example, the monthly survey report. I'm training some of the junior clerks in the office to handle some of the routine things I've been doing and I think I can find time to handle that report.

Harry: You really tempt me, Helen. I'd love to get that thing off my back. It takes so much time . . . and then I could. . . . And you'd take full responsibility for that?

Helen: Yes, Harry, I'm willing to redraft my job description to include the billing and the monthly report. In return I would want a 12 percent raise.

Harry: Twelve percent? Helen, I don't know. It's difficult. . . .

Helen: How about 10 percent and an upgraded title to administrative assistant?

Harry: Helen, you've got a deal.

I think you'll agree that Helen was effective. Let's see why. First, she obviously felt she was worth the money and communicated that. Second, she was able and willing to "blow her own horn" with facts on how her worth had increased. Third, she had prepared her case and decided on some alternatives she could live with. That's the "I" part.

But what else did she do? She empathized with Harry's feelings about being pressured by his people. She had taken the time to think about what Harry might want—to get rid of that annoying report—and pressed her case in those terms. And her approach was not argumentative. Throughout, she maintained a calm, adult approach that made Harry feel more at ease than if she had whined, begged, or demanded.

A TECHNIQUE FOR PROMOTING THE U–I APPROACH

Whenever you enter into a communication with another person, you do more than exchange information. The way you communicate also brings out certain reactions in the other person. We've all seen managers who snarled "hello" at their staff members.

And we've seen others who could criticize a subordinate and have her walk out of the office feeling relatively good about it. These managers, by their words and manner, could make another person feel either good or bad. These are two forms of a very useful communication technique called "stroking."

Stroking is a term that comes out of the transactional analysis approach to human behavior popularized by Eric Berne. According to T.A., a stroke is defined as a sign of recognition. A smile, "hello," a handshake, a kiss are all strokes. So are an insult, "you idiot," a slap, and a kick in the pants. The examples I've given you are of two very different kinds of strokes. The first kind tend to make the receiver feel good; they are called positive strokes. The second kind tend to make the recipient feel bad; those are negative strokes.

STROKING OTHERS

What are the uses of stroking in your job as administrative assistant? You've probably already learned the usefulness of positive strokes for your manager. (Notice how Helen in the last dialog kept using Harry's name, an important positive stroke.) But look more carefully at the kinds of stroking you use with others in your work environment.

To appraise your stroking behavior, write down the names of three people with whom you work or whom you supervise. Set up a sheet of paper with columns headed like this:

Name of Person	*Day*	*Positive Strokes*	*Negative Strokes*	*Relationship Rating*

At the end of each day for a week, fill in the information by writing down the kinds of positive and negative strokes you gave each, then rate your relationship with that person (Good, Fair, Poor). Can you see any correlation between the kinds of strokes you give a person and the resultant relationship? You probably can.

Don't feel bad if you find, through self-analysis, that you give few positive strokes to others. Most of us have grown up in a traditional climate that stresses criticism. From traditional teaching to traditional parenting, the attitude has been: I'll let you know when you do something wrong. Otherwise I won't say anything. Because of that attitude, too many of us are overly attuned to criticism—giving negative strokes. And too often the results are bad feelings and bad relationships.

I'm not suggesting you turn yourself into a little Mary Sunshine, especially if that means trying to stroke people falsely. "What a lovely dress, my dear" can be delivered with all honesty or dripping with sarcasm. But do consider positive stroking as a means of improving relations with someone you don't normally get along with. When was the last time you gave such a person a real compliment?

Stroking your subordinates can be seen as motivation. Stroking customers is good business. Stroking your peers is pure charm. Consider using stroking in all three areas. Whenever you do stroke, keep in mind that "different strokes for different folks" means just that. Some people want to be stroked for their appearance, some for their good ideas, some for their intelligence, some for their persistence. You can tell what a person likes by how he or she responds. And remember, anyone responds to an honest "Thanks," "I like you," or "It's good to have you around."

Some of you may be concerned that directed stroking smacks of manipulation. Whether it's manipulative, I think, depends on your intent. If you give someone a positive stroke and then walk away thinking how smart you are, that's manipulative. But if you walk away feeling good about having given someone a gift (knowing that it increases your chances of getting one, too), that's just good human relations.

STROKING YOURSELF

That last statement, about increasing your chances of getting stroked, brings us to the other half of the equation. So far the uses of stroking we've discussed are part of the U angle. Now to use stroking for the I angle.

When I was a child in school we had an expression we used when any other child was immodest enough to say something nice about herself: "Self-praise stinks." Most of you probably learned something similar when you were young; if so, you probably are still under the power of this strong dictum. But unless you want to be one of those martyrs who spends all her time handing out goodies to others and denying herself, you have to learn to accept positive strokes and to give self-strokes.

I was at a cocktail party a while ago and witnessed a pretty typical scene between two women. One said to the other (sincerely): "That's a beautiful dress." The second woman answered: "Oh, this old thing. . . . I don't look good in blue." What a bombshell of a reply! Not only had the lady in the blue dress succeeded in telling her friend that she was a poor judge of a dress (How could you say it's nice?), she had taken a compliment and turned it into a self-putdown. If you have trouble gaining the respect of others, start monitoring your own behavior to see how often you do this same kind of thing—throw away a positive stroke. Force yourself, if necessary, when receiving a compliment, to say a simple "Thank you." It raises you in the eyes of the other person as well as in your own eyes.

Once you are able to receive strokes, you can go to the next step: initiating self-strokes. Have you ever finished a particularly difficult assignment and, although feeling proud of yourself, yearned for some kind of recognition from others? You can't very well walk up to your boss and ask for a stroke. (It could be dangerous.) Try this instead: "John, here's the Fogler report. It took a lot of juggling to get it just right, and I really feel good about coming up with the right figures." By mentioning your competence (and it must be real, not false bravado) you have reminded the other person of it and thus increased your stature in his eyes.

Stroking can be a powerful tool in promoting both the +U and +I approaches to better interpersonal relationships.

WORKING WITH OTHER WOMEN

I've saved for the end of this chapter one of the biggest problems that exists in offices. It is also one that most people don't want to talk about: the problem of women working with other women. I sometimes wonder if there are more men or more women who insist they would never work for a female boss. It's too easy—and false—to assume that the reason for the eternal conflict of female against female is the basic bitchy nature of women. There are real and very deep-seated reasons for this conflict.

In the first chapter, we talked about the poor self-image many women have because of what they have learned about femaleness. If you learned, when you were young, that a woman is passive, less intelligent, overly emotional, and indecisive, you tend to think of yourself in that way. You also tend to think of *other women* in the same light. Thus a basic lack of respect for other women may be part of our socialization.

Women also tend to denigrate other women for another reason. You probably had an experience like this when you were in high school: You had nothing to do on the upcoming weekend, so you agreed to go to a movie with a girlfriend. Then, at the last minute, a boy called to ask you out, and you just broke off the appointment with your girlfriend. Probably your girlfriend thought you did the right thing too. Why? Because the only really important people were boys. Again, because of the socialization process, many women look on other women as competition for the goodies in life—men.

If you find yourself with negative feelings about working with or for other women, start to change that by becoming aware of the reasons for it. Also work on your self-image. The better you regard yourself, the more you will accept other people, both men and women. Finally, seek out the companionship of women like yourself. You will find they have a lot to offer and you can help each other in the organization.

Looking at this problem from another viewpoint, how can you get other women to regard you with respect? One woman in a seminar asked me how she could best supervise women she was used to working with as co-workers. As a new supervisor, she feared their jealousy and her own inability to gain their respect: I suggested that she start by being aware of the "messages" about women that might be causing her and the others to dislike each other. She might even approach the group and, in one way or another, let them know she realized it was a little awkward for them since they used to work together.

Most important, I suggested she become aware and communicate to her staff that she was now in a position to be helpful to them because of her new role. Being a supervisor, she had the authority to give them needed training, improve their work surroundings, enhance them through recognition, and guide them in their own development.

When you are able and willing to give others what they want, they will accept you.

4

WORKING WITH YOUR MANAGER

or "If I could only change him. . . ."

Your boss can be the greatest aid to your growth, satisfaction, and career—or their greatest barrier. As in many other areas of life, people tend to look at their boss and ascribe "how he is" to a matter of luck. If you're lucky, you've got a good one; if you're not so lucky, it's a struggle. But a good boss–subordinate relationship, like anything else, can be fostered by the right approach. Of course, if you are working for Simon Legree, there are limitations to how much the relationship can be improved. But most relationships between a manager and his assistant can be improved by an application of good problem-solving techniques. Let's look first at difficulties that assistants may have with their managers.

TYPES OF PROBLEM MANAGERS

Traditionalist

This is far and away the most common problem. The traditionalist manager holds that men are leaders and women are followers and never shall they change. He was brought up in the school that said no matter what you call her, the woman who works for you is a handmaiden. Assistants who work for traditionalists find it very difficult to have anything meaningful delegated to them. The traditionalist manager expects his assistant to do what she is told, act as gracious hostess to his guests, look nice, and, if the occasion warrants, salute.

There are still many traditionalists in organizations. Some can be changed and some can't. If you are unhappy with this kind of manager, you will have to decide whether to apply the strategies for change we'll discuss later in the chapter or start looking for a more constructive relationship. If the traditionalist is what you want in a boss, your work life can be very orderly; if he isn't what you want, you will be enduring a great deal of frustration.

Nice Guy

This type of manager has taken a good thing and stretched it a little too far. He has a great command of interpersonal skills, and because of this is very charming. But sometimes he overuses his charm to manipulate you into doing things you really don't want to: "Since you're going to the bank for your own check, I'm sure you wouldn't mind doing a little banking for me. . . ." "My wife really respects your ability and that's why we'd be so happy if you'd be willing to type her term report for her." "I'm just no good at shopping. You women seem to be born with a flair for it. Could you pick up a little something for auntie's birthday this week? She's so hard to please." "Ever since the divorce I've had to learn all kinds of things for myself, but I just can't get the hang of sewing on buttons. Could you. . . ."

Good human relationships are built on the concept of balance. What's good to a certain extent is bad in excess. That's the key to understanding the nice guy. Of course, as an assistant, and I hope friend, to your manager, you will want to be helpful to him. But the assistant to the nice guy finds herself doing too many favors, many on her own time, and begins to resent it. The nice guy can be managed most easily by the simple word "no." Working well with this manager depends on your ability to be clear on what you will and won't do and carrying it through.

Robot

Sometimes this manager is also a traditionalist, but he doesn't have to be. There are some managers who are brilliant at what they do, but the assistants who work for them feel a lack in the job because the manager has so little people orientation. The robot sees everything in analytical terms. Feeling is a word he doesn't recognize. He doesn't stroke, he doesn't have a flair for niceties, and he may be almost insulting in his bluntness at times. You may be having problems with him, but probably most of his subordinates are, too. He may be a technical crackerjack and that's why he's where he is. But he has never learned people skills.

The robot can create a very dull and humorless environment. Whether you choose to work under these conditions depends on the other rewards you get on the job. For example, you may be learning so much from him that it's worth putting up with him. The possibility of his changing depends on how much pressure he gets to change. Are his subordinates rebeling? Does his boss see the problem his lack of people skills creates? When circumstances like these come together the robot manager may be induced to look at expanding his interpersonal skills base.

Dumper

You can learn an awful lot from this manager but you may end up doing his job for him. The manager who gives his assistant a great deal of important work to do is helping her to develop skills she can use in her own career. But the dumper will not be interested in promoting his assistant onward and upward. He has someone who does his job. He retains the title and the salary. Why would he want to lose her? In some cases this manager tells his assistant he is preparing her for his job when he moves up. If that is true he is not a dumper; he is a developer. But if you're doing a great deal of your boss's work, find out where it is leading you.

The four types of managers I've outlined are some of those with whom you may have the most difficulty. Whether you have a manager like one of these or not, they do illustrate an important concept about difficult work relationships: An inability to work well together is a matter of mismatch. The assistant who has problems with her manager, whatever they may be, has expectations about behavior or some aspect of the job that are different from the manager's expectations.

An assistant, for example, may expect her job to be challenging and growth oriented; her traditionalist manager expects her job to be routine and completely supportive to him. If she wanted a routine job there would be no problem. Another assistant expects her job to be pleasant, emotionally satisfying, even fun. Her robot manager expects her to perform the tasks of the role and that is all. If she wanted to be only task oriented, there would be no problem.

A while ago, I gave a presentation to a chapter of the Young Secretaries Association of the National Secretaries Association. When I asked members of the group to talk about their expectations about the job they would seek on graduation, I was surprised to find their expectations so low. Essentially, they wanted a job. It would be nice if they got a few more dollars then they originally thought they would, but they had no perception of the *kind* of manager they wanted to work for.

A few years in the workforce will probably change that drastically. Once you have the opportunity to see the difference in managers, you begin to have preferences. Unfortunately, too many assistants still believe it is a matter of luck or, even worse, that all managers are the same. You have a right—and a responsibility to yourself—to make your work environment what you want. Your work must also fit into your own career aspirations. Once you are clear on that, you will want to check into the areas in which your manager's expectations or behavior do not match yours. Then you can decide on ways to deal with the difficulties you have pinpointed.

MANAGEMENT STYLES

In the last 20 years, a number of models have been designed that attempt to describe the various styles managers have to choose from in doing their jobs. Although the models—and their prescriptions—may differ, they all come down to one thing. A manager has at his disposal two basic areas of behavior—people orientation and task orientation. If we were to chart these two orientations, we would see that, with various combinations of these two factors, there are actually four ways a manager can tend to behave. Look at Figure 3.

According to current management theory, the style a manager chooses depends on his own needs, the expectations of subordinates, and the circumstances. But most managers have a "basic" style they prefer. I'm going to describe four managers based on the four quadrants of the model in Figure 3. My aim is to paint each of these managers as effective in the right time and place. As I talk about each, decide which your manager is most like.

Figure 3: Manager's behavior—people orientation versus task orientation.

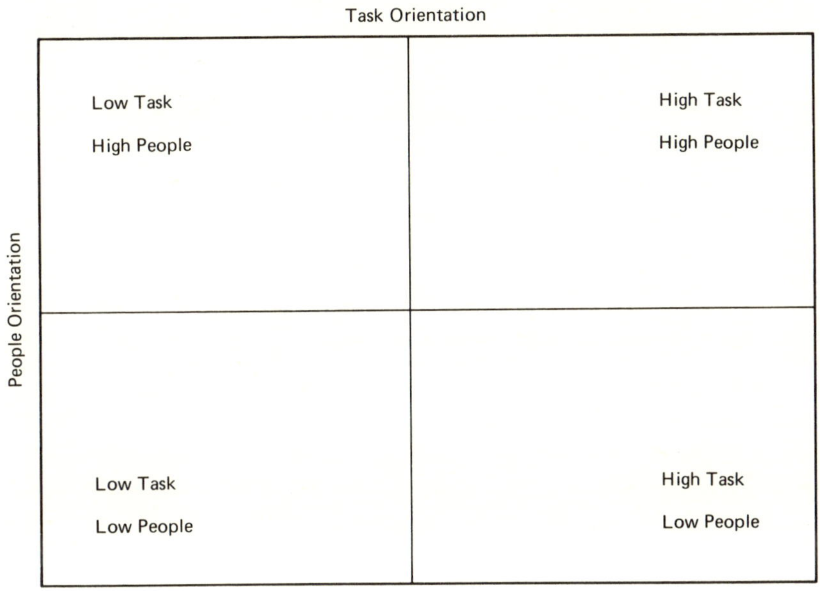

High-Task, Low-People, or Get-the-Job-Done George

George is interested in getting the work done. He tends to be very clear on which way to do it—his way. Because he feels that his way is best he tends to do a lot of telling but little listening. He has little interest in people's feelings. He probably gives little positive feedback to those who report to him. He does not delegate a great deal of responsibility to others but tends, instead, to have his subordinates do bit tasks while he remains responsible for the whole. Those who like a structured environment are usually happy with George.

High-Task, High-People, or Teamwork Tom

This manager has a concern for getting the job done, but his way of doing it involves others. Tom keeps a lot of responsibility for himself but he also delegates. He believes the best way to develop his people is to give them partial responsibility for the work of the department. He has ideas but is also open to the ideas of his subordinates. He will give feedback to his people. Tom has very high expectations of his people and, to be effective working for him, one has to meet those expectatons.

Low-Task, High-People, or Friendly Fred

Fred sees his function as providing the best climate for his subordinates to do their work. His main concern is giving them the support they need to do it. The actual work is delegated to others. He's there to answer questions, give guidance, and give feedback. He may be seen as almost casual to outsiders but can be extremely supportive of his hardworking and able subordinates.

Low-Task, Low-People, or Out-of-the-Way Ollie

Ollie lets the department run itself. That may be because his subordinates are so competent that they can handle it. It may also be because he is often a bureaucrat. In this case the rules and regulations run the department. When surrounded by competent, independent people he can get spectacular results.

ASSISTANT STYLES

In current management theory, each of these styles can be effective when used appropriately. If you are looking to match yourself with your boss's style, the biggest criterion of that match is your own behavioral style as an assistant. Let's use the same basic model to characterize four ways an assistant can prefer to behave vis-à-vis her manager.

High-Task, Low-People, or Structured Sally

Sally works hard and loves it. She gets a great deal of satisfaction from accomplishment. Sally tends to see her work in terms of form and structure. There's a right way to do something and a wrong way. Because Sally is so busy and engrossed with her work, she often has to—or prefers to—work alone.

High-Task, High-People, or We're-All-in-This-Together Wilhemina

This assistant looks for the best of both worlds. Wilhemina gets her work done but also uses people skills in getting help from those around her. She can listen to a directive from her boss but is also capable of making comments and giving opinions when called for. She enjoys the supervision aspect of her job; leading is a strength of hers.

High-People, Low-Task, or Amiable Alice

Alice loves people. She wouldn't work at a job where she couldn't like the people with whom she works. People come before things for Alice, so she sometimes seems lackadaisical about her work. She can get a lot done but she won't be rushed. Her openness and supportive behavior with people make them feel comfortable. She doesn't like to be by herself and prefers to be surrounded with people. She hates being called "the boss."

Low-People, Low-Task, or Avoidance Annie

Annie is out of it, at least in relation to her boss. When a manager practices low-people, low-task behavior appropriately it is because his people can do the job themselves. But when an assistant takes this approach, she is eliminating her very function—to assist. Let's see how the managers and assistants match up. (See Figure 4.)

Two are direct matches. Get-the-Job-Done George and Structured Sally go together very well because they are both essentially inter-

Figure 4: Types of managers and assistants who need to match up.

Match-ups for Managers and Assistants
The Managers

The Assistants	Get-the-Job-Done George	Teamwork Tom	Friendly Fred	Out-of-the-Way Ollie
Most Compatible Assistants	Structured Sally	We're-All-in-This-Together Wilhemina	Amiable Alice Structured Sally	We're-All-in-This-Together Wilhemina Structured Sally
Compatible Assistants	We're-All-in-This-Together Wilhemina	Structured Sally Amiable Alice	We're-All-in-This-Together Wilhemina	Amiable Alice
Assistants to Avoid	Amiable Alice Avoidance Annie	Avoidance Annie	Avoidance Annie	Avoidance Annie

ested in getting the job done. Sally can identify the "right" way as George's. There is no conflict.

Teamwork Tom is a good boss for Wilhemina because he delegates and she accepts. Tom's behavior is a mixture of telling and listening, directing and guiding. Wilhemina is very work oriented but also enjoys the opportunity for input she can experience with this kind of manager.

Friendly Fred may work most effecitvely with one of two kinds of assistants: Amiable Alice or Structured Sally. With Amiable Alice he and she enjoy the same focus. They're both very people oriented. Their office environment may be very pleasant, though not especially productive. When Friendly Fred and Structured Sally become a team, however, an interesting synergy occurs out of their tendency to fill in for each other's deficiencies. When Fred gets too casual, Sally helps keep him on track. As long as she doesn't let his easy-going attitude frustrate her, she can be quite happy working for him and keeping him organized.

Out-of-the Way Ollie requires a real self-starter to be an effective assistant for him. That means either Wilhemina or Sally. Most of the other matches are mildly compatible, but there is one match that is a definite no-no: Amiable Alice and Get-the-Job-Done George. George's "thing" is work and structure. Alice's "thing" is people and support. They tend to get into trouble because George, who, after all, is the manager, gets very involved in output and demanding of ways and means. Alice can't understand someone like that because output just isn't that important to her. George tends to think Alice is flighty; Alice thinks George is a dictator. They probably won't stay together very long.

THE PROBLEM-SOLVING APPROACH

The concept of matches is very useful to give you a general idea of the basis for compatible and incompatible manager–assistant teams. To characterize yourself and your boss according to this model and see how you fit together can be a good first step. But it isn't enough. If you feel that you and your manager experience too many conflicts in your daily work together, you have to take a problem-solving approach to accomplish any change.

Let us say, for example, that you have identified yourself as We're-All-in-This-Together Wilhemina and your manager as Get-the-

Job-Done George. You are work and people oriented. Your manager is work oriented. This is one of the matches that is mildly compatible, neither the best nor the worst. You feel you and he could be more effective together. Where do you go from there? You follow the five problem-solving steps.

Isolate the problem.
Decide what you want.
Think of alternative ways to get it.
Decide on the best alternative.
Try it out.

Let me take you through the process with Wilhemina and George. Wilhemina is doing the thinking.

Isolate the Problem

What is really happening? Well, George makes all the decisions by himself. When I started the job that was fine, because I didn't know the work of the department. But now I could be more valuable to him with my input on things. One good example is telling me exactly how to do the monthly report—every month. I think it should be overhauled to be more useful, but he never asks for my ideas. I'd like to be asked what I think sometimes. I know a lot about people—I'm a pretty good observer. And I could really give him some hints on how to get through to his own people. I'd also like him to trust me more and let me find my own way. Not completely, mind you, because I respect George's ability and knowledge, but more than now.

Decide What You Want

I want more freedom. I want an opportunity to build some flexibility into the job. I'd also like to keep some of the things I like about the job. The salary is good, the office staff is great, the area is a good one for learning.

Think of Alternative Ways to Get It

I'll make a list of possible alternatives:

1. I could change jobs—inside the company or out.
2. I could try to change George, talk to him directly and ask him to consider amending my job description.

3. I could start hinting at the fact that I'm unhappy and see if he can sense the problem.
4. I could do some things on my own without telling him and just see how he reacts.
5. I could do nothing, considering that I'm not extremely dissatisfied, and wait to see what happens.

Decide on the Best Alternative

First, I think I'll eliminate alternative 1. Except for this aspect, I really like my job. I don't think I'm ready to change yet. I'll also eliminate 5. I'd feel better if at least I knew I tried to do something about the situation. Alternative 3 is a little too indirect for me. Didn't I read that book on assertiveness? It said hinting and hoping were copouts. That leaves 2 or 4. Alternative 4 is risky. George is pretty clear on what he wants, and if I change it without telling him he may get very defensive, and that won't do me any good.

Alternative 2 is risky, too, but it's not underhanded. It's out in the open. The worst that could happen is that he would fire me. But he won't do that. He's structured; not unreasonable. I'll just have to approach him in the right way. Maybe I could use 4 as a backup in case he hesitates or waffles—sort of get him used to more input from me gradually. Yes, I think I'm going to have to talk to George.

Try It Out

Tomorrow afternoon, when it's not too busy, I'm going to talk to George. I'll pre-prepare a modified job description as a base for discussion and practice up on some of those assertiveness techniques. I feel better already.

That example will give you the idea. So many ineffective interpersonal relationships are put down to "personality conflicts." That's a dead end, because you can't actually change personalities. But you can change some of other people's behavior—by changing your own. In this case, that means opening up dialog on a subject that has been put aside too long. Later in the chapter we'll look at some specific ways you can change the boss.

GETTING ALONG

A good manager–assistant relationship is like a good marrriage—and no sexual connotations are intended. How are these relationships similar? They are based on similar goals, open communication, trust and respect, and a willingness to work out difficulties.

Similar goals mean that both the manager and the assistant find that by working together they can achieve their individual goals better than by working alone. The manager's job and career aspirations should be helped along by an effective assistant. The assistant must see her own objectives satisfied, too, so that they both grow and become what they want.

Two people working together cannot have goals in concert unless they are willing to talk about them. This ranges from being clear each day on each other's job priorities to an understanding of where the other person wants to go in the organization.

Trust and respect are not automatic; they are an end result of the interactions of two people. If an assistant shows by her actions that she can be trusted to do what she says she will do, she will be treated as trustworthy. If a manager shows that he is open and honest in his dealings with those around him, he will be seen as worthy of respect by his assistant.

We are living in an era of "creative divorce," "creative labor relations," and "creative parent–child relationships." All these imply is that relationships must be worked out: that before a couple separates, or a union strikes a company, or a parent and child reach an impasse, they owe each other the willingness to work at settling their differences. It's the same between a manager and his assistant. I've put together some hints to help you get along better with your manager and avoid sudden disruptive conflicts.

Be Clear on What Your Job Is

There's no better way to be in constant conflict with your manager than to be working at cross-purposes with him. "But I thought you wanted me to. . . ." "But I thought my job was. . . ." "But any assistant would know that. . . ." These types of discussions indicate that neither of you is clear on what you are expected to do. Sit down and negotiate a working job description—and be prepared to amend it as your work changes.

Don't Get Hung Up on Individual Quirks

Your manager is a human being with certain ways of behaving. Some of these are *different* from what you would choose, but not necessarily a barrier to your working together effectively. If he's a stickler for detail, can you live with it instead of letting it get to you ten times a day? If you can't stand his choice of ties, does that really affect the ability he has as a manager? An amiable, people-oriented assistant trying to work with a very structured and task-oriented manager has real problems to sort out. But don't put energy into trying to change parts of your manager that are not important to your relationship.

I once had a manager tell me that he had a habit of swearing when things got rough in his job. When he interviewed a prospective assistant, he said, he purposely used some of his "ripe" language because he didn't intend to change and he didn't want to be surrounded by someone who was continually flinching at his words. To me that's a quirk and the assistant has to choose whether she wants to live with it or not.

Maintain Balance Between Being a Martyr and an Egoist

In a number of places in this book, I talk about balancing one's behavior between undesirable, ineffective extremes. Just so, in your working relationship with your manager, you must walk a tightrope between being a martyr and being an egoist. The martyr assistant "takes" any kind of behavior her manager dishes out. He can insult her, he can deprive her, he can overwork her, he can call her cutesy names, he can ask her to shine his shoes, and she will comply. That's not an effective relationship; that's slavery. Eventually both will suffer from the bad feelings and resentments that arise.

On the other hand, there have been a number of stories in newspapers the last few years about secretaries and assistants who would not do certain parts of the job their managers expected and were fired because of it. Some sued and won their cases. I think you are the one who must decide what you will do on a job and make sure your boss understands that. But just as the martyr assistant goes too far in putting down her own needs, the egoist assistant may go too far in promoting her needs only. Sometimes you have to work late; sometimes you may have to do a favor for your boss. Without a certain amount of giving the relationship will never be ideally effective.

Be Competent

Your job is to get your boss promoted—or at least to help him be extremely effective in doing his job. Do what you say you will to the best of your ability. Support your manager publicly. Bring all the resources you have to the job. If you've worked out a good, clear relationship you will receive the rewards, too.

Find Out What's Important to Your Manager

I don't mean find out what your job is. I mean find out those little things that can never really be written down anywhere but that are extremely important to him. You may have a wonderful, analytical mind and put together well-documented reports, but if you're a lousy speller and he can't stand that, you will not be seen as effective to him. If you keep the inventory of office supplies in perfect order but he can never find his favorite erasers, it will bother him constantly.

Never Surprise the Manager

Primary functions of the assistant are to anticipate, prepare, follow up. You are a vital communications link between your manager and the rest of the organization. Keep him abreast of things. You will never be forgiven if you could have helped him to avoid ending up with "egg on his face" and you didn't.

If you keep in mind the marriage analogy and these guidelines, your general rapport with your manager should improve. But what about those instances when you decide you want to change your situation? If you see some aspect of your boss's behavior as a great barrier to your joint effectiveness, you have three major alternatives: live with it, change it, or leave it.

You may decide to live with it when the chances of changing your manager are small because of his age, deep-seated attitudes, and general personality. *Don't* take this alternative until you have tried to pursue some change. Otherwise you may be assuming he can't change when he can and will. You may find you choose to live with the situation because you find other parts of the job very satisfying and therefore want to stay with it.

You may attempt to change the manager's behavior. As far as I am concerned, this is the ideal solution, and certainly the first step before either living with it or leaving it.

You may leave the situation, transfer, take a new job, start a new career. Sometimes this is the most extreme and most risky path to follow. It can also be the best. After all, sometimes divorce is the best answer to a rocky marriage.

HOW TO CHANGE THE BOSS

Shoulder at Least Part of the Responsibility

People tend to get into habitual ways of dealing with each other. You do A, I do B, you do C, I do D, and so on. If you want me to stop giving you a B you must stop giving me an A. That means you have to change your own behavior first. If you would prefer that I stop taking up your time with a lot of small talk, you have to stop sitting there so attentively. Do something else to lead me to a new behavior.

Bring It Out into the Open

"John, I'd like to talk to you about our use of the files." If John messes up your files, don't just have a tantrum every time he does and expect anything to be different. Bring it out, talk about it, but remember the next rule.

Relate the Change to Better Results

Why should your manager change his behavior? Because you want him to? That's not a very motivating force. Instead, relate the new behavior you want to the promise of a better result: "If the files are accessible to everyone, they tend to get mislaid. If I'm in charge of them, I will keep track of them. That way a great deal of time will not be wasted looking for them when we really need them."

See Your Boss as a Person

Your boss is not a god, not your father, not all-knowing, not all-caring—just a human being like you. He does what he does because that's what he has learned in life. Now you come along and say "Change." Help; don't push. Suggest; don't demand. Ask for what you want; don't wait and hope.

Use Good Human Relations in Your Change Management

Most people make a big fuss about what they don't want and quietly and smugly accept what they do. That's a mistake. Instead of complaining when you don't get something you want, be prepared to reinforce what you want. "Thank you for inviting me to that special meeting. I feel I learned a lot that I can use in my work." "I appreciate you leaving me alone to work quietly on that project. It really required concentration." "Thank you for understanding my position." These are examples of the technique called positive reinforcement—giving feedback for desirable behavior.

Contrast that with the average approach, commenting only on undesirable behavior: "I wish you'd invite me to some of those meetings. I need the exposure." "How can I get this work done with all those interruptions?" "You never understand me."

The trick, if you will, is to present the possible new behavior to the other person in the terms we've discussed. Then every time he approximates that new behavior, you give him attention as a reward for doing it. Psychologically it makes the other person want to continue the new behavior.

Beware of making people defensive, of making your manager feel "bad" because he won't do something you want. A person who feels pushed against the wall will usually give you nothing. Concentrate on "I" phrases (I feel I am capable of doing this project on my own.) instead of "you" phrases (Why don't you ever give me a project to do on my own?). The chapter on assertiveness and other special techniques will elucidate on these approaches.

Put the Odds in Your Favor

If you're about to ask your manager to consider changing something about your job or his behavior, choose the time. Your manager should be in a relaxed mood. If possible, it should be after a successful project on your part. Feel comfortable with yourself and your request and you will make the other person feel that way too.

CHOOSING A BOSS

Your boss is one of the most important elements in your career success. If you are at a point in your life when you are looking for a new position, be prepared to *choose* the situation (read "boss") that will make your working life as pleasant and rewarding as possible.

1. Find out what the job entails. Ask to see a job description. Tell your prospective employer what your understanding of the job is. Clarify what you will be expected to do—especially if you have strong feelings about not wanting to do certain things.

2. Know what your style tends to be and try to characterize your prospective manager's style. As you talk to him ask yourself what life

would be like working with him. You are looking for the best possible match.

3. Tune into your intuitive feelings about your prospective new boss. Do you feel comfortable with him? Do you trust him? Do you respect him? Will he be open and flexible enough?

BRING IT ALL TOGETHER

This chapter has been about improving your relationship with your manager. The underlying assumption has been that there is no such thing as a "good" or "bad" boss, nor are there "good" or "bad" assistants. There are relationships that work and those that don't. You have a great deal of input into making the kind of relationship you want.

The biggest barrier on the assistant's part to good manager–assistant relationships is a feeling of powerlessness. You either get blessed with a good boss or stuck with a bad one. Chapter 1 talked about personal barriers to effectiveness; a sense of inability to control the situation can be a major deterrent to your effectiveness and growth.

To end this chapter I'd like to relate a true story. An assistant was telling me about her first day at work with her present manager. She was sitting at her new desk getting used to things when he called her into the office: "Hey, Tiger, come in here." She entered his office not sure it was she that he had called and said: "Tiger?" "Sure," he replied, "I always call my girl Tiger." She said, "I prefer to be called by name. Would you please call me Roberta?" "Oh, of course," he said, somewhat surprised. They went on with their work. She's still with him and they have a fine working relationship—over which she has a great deal of control.

5

MANAGING YOUR MOST IMPORTANT RESOURCE

or "If I only had time. . . ."

A FABLE

Once upon a time a young woman took a job in a factory. On her first day, her supervisor explained to her what the job would be:

> "Now, what you have to do is sit here in front of this conveyer belt. You can see that every once in a while a bucket is going to pass in front of you. These buckets are empty and your job is to fill them. You'll notice that you have two piles on either side of your chair. That's what you fill the buckets with. This first pile is pure substance; it's quite heavy. The other pile contains the same substance mixed with dirt; it's not so heavy. What you do. . . ."
>
> Unfortunately, at this point the supervisor was suddenly called away. "Just get started," he told her. "I'll be back later to see if you've got the hang of it."
>
> Our heroine sat down at the conveyer belt and started to fill each bucket. Not knowing which pile she should choose from, she'd sometimes scoop from one pile, sometimes from the other. She tended to scoop more from the mixed pile because it was easier. As time passed she got tired and often let some buckets pass empty in front of her. "What's the difference," she thought, "there are so many."

> Finally the supervisor returned to finish his explanation. This is when she found out that her pay was to be adjusted according to how many buckets she filled and with what. Each bucket filled with the mixed substance was worth *X* dollars to her. A bucket full of pure substance paid twice as much, and empty buckets paid her nothing.

What does this little story have to do with you? Everything. Because each of you—everyone in the world—has the same opportunity to gain or lose as the woman in the story. The "buckets" are minutes. What we have to fill them with are either useful, valuable actions that pay a great deal or less valuable actions that pay less. Just as the woman in the story would sometimes let empty buckets pass by her, so all of us let minutes, and even hours, pass by unfilled. Our payment for this unfilled time is . . . zero.

Time management, in its best sense, is life management. We'll be looking more closely at this in Chapter 10. Here, our concern is time on the job and how best to use it. Our aim on the job is to fill as much of our time as possible with activity that will pay us back the highest rewards. Interestingly, time management is one of those subjects that seems to be of great concern to every level of management. Assistants, supervisors, managers, and even CEOs want to get more out of each working day. Assistants, especially, need to manage their time well because they are often responsible for organizing their manager's time as well as their own.

We're going to look at time management in this chapter from the viewpoint of a system I've developed. If you follow the system, you *will* get more out of your day. And we'll also be looking at how you can help your manager use his time more effectively. But first, let's clear up some of the misconceptions people have about time management.

MYTHS OF TIME MANAGEMENT

Myth No. 1. With better time management, you will be able to "find" new time during the day.

Truth. From the day we are born to the day we die, we each have the same number of hours per day—24. Some people seem to have more. This is because they manage their time better. The only place you can "find" time for a given activity is by taking it away from some other activity. For example, you spend four hours a week filing and one hour a week training clerks. You feel the training deserves more time. By using awareness, planning, and time tricks, you may be able to do the filing in three hours; you now have two hours for the training.

Myth No. 2. Effective time management is exactly the same for everyone.

Truth. Each person has different priorities, different needs, different personalities. That is why in this discussion of time management we will often give you a choice in any given area on how to use your time better. The principles are the same; the application must be individualized. For example, telephone interruptions may be a large time waster for one person—one who has a great deal of detail work to do. But for the assistant to a customer service manager who may have to handle many customer calls, the telephone has a high priority.

Myth No. 3. Activity is good in itself.

Truth. There are too many "chickens with their heads cut off" running around organizations. We've all known people who could look busy but never accomplished anything. If this myth were true, it would be beneficial to eliminate lunch, coffee breaks, meditation time, and anything else that didn't produce tangible results. That would be absurd. The truth is that only activity—or inactivity—related to one's goals is useful. A "time nut" is not necessarily effective.

Myth No. 4. Time management is a complex subject to learn.

Truth. In only one chapter in this book, I can show you the basics of effective time management. It's not a lack of knowledge that keeps people from managing their time. This leads us to the final, and most devastating, myth.

Myth No. 5. Once you know the basics of time management, you will automatically make better use of your time.

Truth. Time management does not "take," like a vaccination. More than anything else, the successful use of time will depend on what you do with it after you learn it. Each morning when we wake up we are faced with a choice: Will we use this day in a way that enriches our lives or will we waste it? And each day we have exactly the same opportunity.

THE LIST APPROACH TO BETTER TIME MANAGEMENT

I have always found that the best way to teach people is usually the simplest. For that reason, I've developed a simple system for improving time use; it's called LIST. LIST is an acronym for four important areas of time management with which you must deal to make better use of your time. The meanings are as follows:

Log
Identification of time wasters and opportunities
System
Tricks

Now let's find you some more time.

A DIAGNOSTIC STEP

The first letter of LIST refers to the use of a time log. Those who try making a log typically find the experience "horrible," "frustrating," and even "time-consuming." Why, then, do I suggest it? Because there is no better way for you to start to manage your time than to find out what you're doing with it right now.

If you ever set out to change something about yourself—to stop smoking, to lose weight, to budget your money better—and you consulted an expert in any one of these areas, the expert probably told you this: For the first week, don't change anything. Just keep a record of what you do. So you started writing down how many, and when, and under what circumstances you picked up a cigarette. You wrote down everything you ate. You kept notes on where you spent every cent. At the end of the diagnostic period, you looked at your record and usually came to two types of conclusions:

1. I don't believe I smoke that much—eat that much—spend that much.
2. I seem to pick up a cigarette whenever I have coffee. I eat most at night. I spend a lot of money on restaurant meals.

In other words, you were able to find out the extent of the activity you wanted to change as well as to find out the conditions under which you carried it out.

It's exactly the same way with time management. I guarantee you that if you keep a log for only one week and summarize the results, you will look at them and say: "I don't believe I spend that much time on the phone," "I don't believe I spend that little time on training," or even "I don't really know what I did with that much time."

HOW TO DO A LOG

There are a number of ways you can do a time log. Two examples are in Figure 5. Using Example 1, you start each day with a paper on which you have listed 15-minute time segments. Each time you start a new activity, you write it in the proper time slot. To use Example 2, you estimate beforehand what your major activities will be, draw up corresponding columns, and check off the appropriate time used every 15 minutes. Either log can be divided into 10-minute or half-hour segments if they are more appropriate to your job. Any log should be kept for a minimum of five days to give you an accurate sample.

Figure 5: Two possible time logs for time management.

9:00
9:15
9:30
9:45
10:00
etc.

Example 1

	Filing	Typing	Supervision	etc.
9:00				
9:15				
9:30				
9:45				
10:00				
etc.				

Example 2

If the prospect of five days of tracking your time seems unbearable, I can suggest one way around that. Do one day a week for five weeks—Monday one week, Tuesday the next week, and so on. Most jobs are similar enough over the weeks to give you accurate results with that system. Once you have completed a five-day log, summarize the time use on each activity. For example, in one 35-hour week, you divided your time by:

Report writing, 3 hours
Talking on phone, 5 hours
Filing, 3 hours
Typing, 5 hours
Dictation, 3 hours
and so on

YOUR PERSONAL BALANCE SHEET

You now know where your time goes. The next thing you want to look at is relative time use. To do this, take another sheet of paper and write down two headings: on the left, Things I Spend Too Much Time On (Time Wasters); on the right, Things I Spend Too Little Time On (Opportunities). Using your summary as a source of information, fill in those items on the left that seem to be taking too much time; these are your personal time wasters.

Let's take a moment to clarify that last term. A time waster can be, but rarely is, something you shouldn't be doing at all. More commonly it is that type of activity that seems to take too much time for the payoff it gives you. You are talking about time wasters when you say: "If I could just shut off the telephone once in a while." "Why do people keep interrupting me?" "Isn't there a faster way to file?"

On the right-hand side of your page, put down the activities on which you feel you are spending too little time. Often, these items can be ignored for a while without consequences, but can mushroom into large problems. Examples of these are training of subordinates, creative work on improvements in work methods, and special self-improvement projects. Here is a sample balance sheet:

Too Much Time	*Too Little Time*
Filing	Working on new system
Greeting visitors	Training
Taking dictation	Planning with manager

Your balance sheet gives you direction in planning your improved use of time. Your opportunities are your motivation; they're what you want the time for. Your time wasters are where you'll be getting that time by shaving off wasted minutes.

If you are just reading this chapter through and have not yet done a time log, it would be useful to take a moment out here and write an estimated version of your balance sheet. Most people already have an idea of what their major time wasters are and where their time should be going.

So far, the LIST system has been diagnostic: the use of a log to identify time wasters and time opportunities. The next part is the solution, which has two aspects: systematizing your use of time and incorporating tricks of time use.

USING A SYSTEM

About a year ago a woman in a seminar, while we were talking about the use of time to reach one's goals, mentioned she was studying Spanish. She went on to say that her husband was learning French and carpentry. "How interesting," I said, "that you're using your leisure time in such engrossing hobbies." "No," she replied, "they're not hobbies. It's for our trip." She went on to explain that she and her husband had plans for ten years in the future, when the children were grown. They were going to leave their jobs and travel around the world. They were each learning languages and useful skills to use on that trip. Rarely have I met anyone who was so carefully investing her time toward reaching her goals.

Not everyone wants to plan her time so precisely, but all of us can use the same principle. In fact, there are two aspects to this third part of LIST, a system based on (1) outlining your weekly goals once a week and (2) preparing a daily To-Do list. At the beginning of each week, take some time to write down what you want to accomplish that week. List these in terms of results, not activities. For example, there is an enormous difference between saying you want to work on the semiannual report and saying you want to prepare a draft for the semiannual report. The latter statement causes you to think in terms of, and work toward, an end result.

Be sure to include in your weekly goals items that are important to you but not yet urgent. Let me illustrate. In January your tax return is important but not urgent, so you put off doing it. By the time April rolls around, the tax return has moved into the *urgent* category and you may find yourself running around getting documents and having it done. If you had taken a little bit of time each month it wouldn't have been such a hassle to get it done. In the same way, when you write your weekly goals, include at least one area that may get out of control if you don't pay attention to it. Training subordinates, learning how to use a new machine, doing some work on a big, not-yet-due project are all examples of such items.

Fill in your weekly calendar from this list of goals. And don't forget to take advantage of your own special situation to accomplish things most effectively. For example, slot in the heavy detail work during times of the day when you usually get the fewest phone calls.

PICKING OUT THE MOST IMPORTANT

The daily To-Do list is the second part of the system in LIST. First, I'd like to show you how it shouldn't be done. Let's look in on an administrative assistant who had just been introduced to the concept of a daily To-Do list. Here's how she did it. She sat down first thing in the morning and wrote down everything she wanted to accomplish that day. In fact, she wrote down a large number of things. Then she looked at the list and tried to decide where to start. "Straighten my desk," she said. "That will give me a clear place to work, and I've been promising myself I would for a couple of days." After spending half an hour on that, she looked at her list again. This time, she chose filing. "I like to get it out of the way," she told herself. Let's skip to the next scene. It's about 4 o'clock and our assistant is trying to finish some urgent work that must be completed by the end of the day. "Guess I'll have to stay late tonight. That time management stuff isn't very useful, is it?"

This example illustrates the major problem that people encounter when they first start doing a daily To-Do list: a failure to set priorities. Without that step you might as well put your list on the wall and throw darts at it to determine what you should be doing at any given time. Setting priorities is based on a rule that is sometimes called Pareto's Principle, or the 80/20 rule. According to this rule, in any given group of items, a relatively small percentage of the items is responsible for a relatively large percentage of the return. You get 80 percent of the value of a newspaper from 20 percent of the newspaper (front page, editorial, comics, sports). Your company gets 80 percent of its sales from 20 percent of its customers. You get 80 percent of the value of your day from 20 percent of your activities.

To illustrate this for yourself, list 10 activities you carry out each day. Now take the same 10 activities and put them in priority order. According to Pareto's Principle, if you do just the top two items, you will get back 80 percent of your payoff for the day. "Ah," you say, "that would be nice if I made those kinds of decisions, but it's my manager who makes—and often changes—the priorities of the day." That's why, for the assistant, the daily To-Do list should be prepared *with* her manager.

THE MORNING CONFERENCE

Up to now, everything we've said about time management can be used by you or your manager to get more out of the workday. Here we're going to look at the issue of joint time management.

For an assistant, the key to better time management for herself and her manager is the morning conference. If the assistant doesn't know what the priorities of the day are, it is almost impossible for her to plan to get the important things done. The "report has to be done today" given to you at 3:30, the mad dash to get together material for a meeting, the excessive overtime, the hassles between manager and assistant—all can result from skipping that important morning meeting. At the meeting the manager can use his own To-Do list to show you how you can help with his priorities that day. That way you can plan for his needs as well as your own.

Incidentally, if this discussion of the early morning conference has led you to throw up your hands because you know your manager doesn't work that way, don't despair. Many assistants do not have morning conferences. But I hope you will try to initiate these meetings. Use your own time log to show your manager where you may be wasting time because you are unclear on priorities. Show him how careful planning will allow you to take more off his shoulders. This approach will tend to motivate him to try something new. Just beware of using the approach, "I know what our time problem is. You." It will only cause your manager to become defensive.

TRICKS OF TIME USE

Everyone develops individual ways of doing things faster on the job. You probably have some tricks of your own. I'd like to share with you some of the time tricks for managers and assistants I have collected from assistants. If any given activity is taking up too much time, there are essentially three ways you can get better time use out of it: eliminate it completely, delegate it, or do it a faster way. Most time wasters will be handled by the last.

Ways You Can Help Your Manager Save Time

Interruptions. Get people to make an appointment. If they don't have one, be assertive about refusing them entry. To avoid getting a reputation as a watchdog, you should ask your manager to back you up, either formally or informally, whenever someone without an appointment barges in: "As Helen told you, this is a bad time for me to see you. Could we get together after lunch? Just ask her to make a note of it."

It is even possible to "train" people to come at certain times without being too heavy-handed. For example, a salesman who visits regularly shows up one day wanting to see your boss. You tell him that's not possible but suggest: "Since I know he'd want to see you, why not stop by next week? Tuesday and Thursday afternoon are good times." That way you're encouraging a visitor to come at a time more convenient to your manager, but you're doing it without brushing off the visitor or giving yourself a reputation as a dragon lady.

Scheduled Visitors. Prepare material beforehand that your manager will need to meet with a visitor. Work out a general agreement with your manager that you will interrupt after a certain period of time he spends with any visitor. That way the manager can end the conversation if he wants the plea of "another appointment" or ask you to "hold that other appointment" if he wants to continue.

Mail. Screen and set priorities on incoming mail. Handle whatever you can. Put aside the "temptation mail" (junk mail, brochures, magazines, and other mail that is interesting but unimportant) for a time when the manager can go through it quickly. Reading this mail can even serve as a reward after a difficult task.

You can save your manager's time on outgoing mail by taking over as much of it as possible. Suggest he give you guidelines and you write the actual letter. It's a good learning experience for you and a time saver for him.

Dictation. Use a dictating machine. Personal dictation wastes too much time for both of you. If your manager resists, perhaps you can work out a compromise: dictating machine for long reports; personal dictating for letters, for example.

Telephone. To screen or not depends on your situation. Some companies want their executives to answer their own phones; some demand just the opposite. If you have no such constraints, you and your manager will want to decide which is best. Have your manager keep a telephone log for a week: the caller, the subject of the call, and who (you or your manager) handled it. If the manager has to handle most of the calls, it's a waste of your time to answer his phone. If you handle a lot, you should screen.

In general, the more calls you can handle, the more you will save your manager's time. To do this requires a joint effort on both your parts. The manager must be willing to let you handle certain calls; you must assertively insist to the caller that you can. If your manager is the type of person who tends to get stuck on the phone and wants to change that, buy him an "executive egg timer" for Christmas; he can shoot for three minutes a call.

Meetings. Suggest to your manager that having a stopping time as well as a starting time on the meeting memo will prepare the attendees to finish within that time. Alert people before the meeting to remind them what they are expected to bring in terms of information, finished work, and so on. After the meeting, use follow-up to remind people of the commitments they have made.

Procrastination. Help your manager to avoid procrastinating by reminding him before things are due so he gets around to doing them. You might offer to do parts of a big project to give him momentum.

Ways You Can Save Your Own Time

Take time to save time. Give yourself self-development projects periodically to improve long-term time use. For example, if you work on improving your spelling, you will eventually save retyping time.

Don't waste time on useless emotions. If you hate to do something, either get it changed or live with it without griping. The more you gripe, the more time you waste.

Keep your finger on the future. Maintain a tickler file arranged month by month. In here you can put reminders about doing certain projects or even write yourself useful notes. For example, after the annual Christmas party that you arranged, write a "report" on what went well and what should have been different. Put it in the tickler file for next fall. When you come to plan the party for next year, you will have your guidelines all written out for yourself.

Use time patterns. Find out when people tend to be in their offices and use that time to make phone calls. Determine your own prime time, too. That's the time of day when you feel at your best. If you're a "morning person," do your most difficult work then. If you feel your best in the afternoon, schedule your most demanding work then. Either way, you'll get more done.

Don't be a go-fer. Convince your boss that it is a waste of time for both of you if he constantly interrupts you. He can leave notes in his out box instead of buzzing you every few minutes, or agree to make only hourly interruptions.

Set up systems to avoid interruptions. You might put together an in–out board for everyone in the department, showing where they can be reached when away from their desk or out of town. Keep individual boxes for people in the department where they can pick up their messages instead of bothering you. Remember, though, that when you are introducing any new idea you have to take time to show how it works and how it will benefit those who will be using it.

Group and plan. Do a number of similar activities together to save time. Making phone calls and photocopying are good places to apply this time rule.

Learn to say no. If being agreeable is making you harried, do something about it. Start asserting your own needs when too many people ask for too much.

Extend yourself. Use time management principles in your non-work life. Make a To-Do list, for example, on Saturday morning and reward yourself for finishing it by doing something you want on Saturday afternoon.

More than One Boss

Many secretaries/assistants these days have more than one manager. If this is your situation, the principles of time management are the same—or even more important. Check with each manager in the morning so you will know his priorities for the day. If caught between two people's priorities, ask the managers themselves to make a decision on which should be done first. You can't do two things at once, and you can't decide between two managers without offending one of them.

YOUR CHOICE

Time is one of the few areas in life in which we are all exactly equal. We each have 24 hours a day to accomplish what we want in life. Some people do seem to get more out of their time; they see time as a precious resource and use it accordingly. Why not start using LIST and become one of those people?

6

BASIC COMMUNICATIONS

or "Huh?"

Many people in management focus on communication as one of the most important skills they use—and one of the most difficult to learn. When an administrative assistant says she has a communication problem, what does she mean? She could mean a variety of things. Let's look at some examples.

"My boss and I don't seem to communicate very well."

Often, what she really means is that they don't talk at all. She may want more responsibilities in her job, for example, but is not gettting them from her manager. She sees him as unresponsive to her needs; he sees her as vaguely dissatisfied and wonders why. The situation may continue this way in a nonproductive stalemate, or eventually it may move into a "separation." The communication problem here is that no one is doing any talking or listening.

"If they just did what I told them to do there'd be no problems."

Telling is a valid form of communication. It is fast, direct, easy to do—and limited in effectiveness. If, for example, an assistant keeps telling the junior people in the office what to do but doesn't get the results she wants, it may be because the form of communication she uses doesn't really get the message across or produces bad feelings when it does.

"That other department doesn't know how to communicate with us."

The implication here is that lack of understanding between two people—or two groups—is the other's fault. In reality, the assistant in this case may be in the habit of sending out memos to the other department full of jargonistic words and phrases that are very clear to her and her department but as foreign as another language to the other department. Communication can go wrong in many ways. It's a wonder that people communicate at all.

In the past few years, communication has been dissected and analyzed as a very intricate process. Let's look at a simpler approach to breaking down the communication process and see all the factors that go into communication breakdown.

We will start with two people, A and B. Person A gets an idea in her head: ★. She decides to communicate that idea to the second person, but since she can't transfer the idea directly, she must put it into a form that is transmittable. So person A translates her original idea—or codes it—into a word that can be expressed: star.

Person A then chooses a mode of transmission. Should she write it or say it? She chooses to speak the word. The sound of the word travels through the air to person B. Person B has to have some way to receive the word. Since it is spoken, she receives it with her ears.

In her mind person B takes the symbol or word and processes it back—decodes it—to an idea. If everything in the process has gone well, we will end up with both A and B having this ★ in their heads.

But there are many elements in the process that can go wrong. What if the original idea that person A had in her mind wasn't very clear? It would be difficult for her to express it in a clear way to the other person. Or what if the symbol she chose could represent many things? Her listener might not know which one she meant if she didn't explain it.

The mode of transmission could make a difference. Did person A say it so softly that person B couldn't hear it, or so loudly that person B was offended and didn't *want* to hear it?

The surrounding environment could be interfering with the communication. Maybe there are noisy machines, people talking, distractions that cause person A to be inaudible or person B not to hear. The word might be lost.

Or what if our receiver is not "in good working order"? She has a hearing difficulty, for example. Or maybe she doesn't like person A and deliberately shuts out anything she is saying.

Person B might receive the word but, in decoding it, have difficulty deciding which of many meanings Person A really intended. And we might end up with a ridiculous miscommunication like this:

> A: Would you draw me a star? (★)
> B: That's too difficult. (Paul Newman)
> A: (She's crazy.)

Unless person A checks with person B to see that they mean the same thing, the communication is completely messed up.

All these problems had to do with only one word. Now you see why communication is so difficult. All the things that can go wrong in the communication process are reviewed in Figure 6.

If this concept seems too simplistic to you, think about this news item that appeared recently in my local newspaper. The report told about an inquiry into a near plane crash at a large city airport. As a

Figure 6: Possible pitfalls in the communication process.

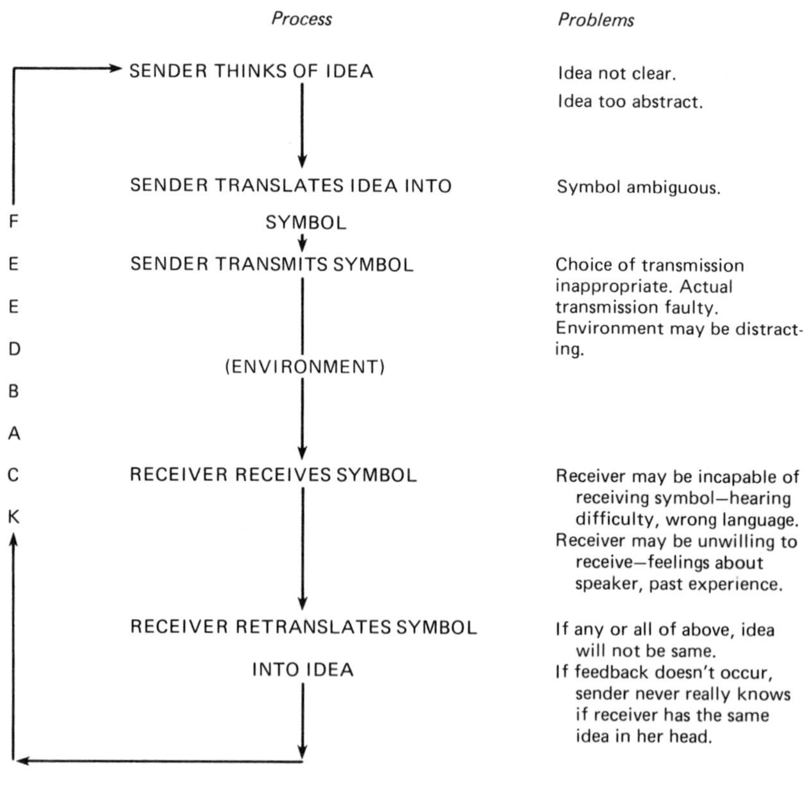

727 descended to land, the pilot saw a snowplow on the runway and narrowly averted crashing into it. During the inquiry, what had happened became obvious. As the plane descended, the tower told the driver of the snowplow to "clear the runway." He started to do just that—clearing off the snow. What the tower meant, of course, was to get off the runway. All this over one word.

Now that we have seen how the communication process can go wrong, we're going to look at improving communication from the viewpoint of both the sender and the receiver: How can you talk and listen more effectively?

SENDING COMMUNICATIONS

As the sender of a communication, you have the difficult job of taking an idea that is in your head and getting it—without benefit of ESP—into another person's head. To help you "transplant" your ideas better, I've put together some guidelines for the more effective sending of communications.

Think First

Most people look on their communications style as something that is as basic a part of themselves as the color of their eyes or the length of their body—predetermined and unchangeable. To be a better communicator requires you to accept the fact that you have learned to communicate in certain ways throughout your life and can, therefore, unlearn those and relearn new ways if you choose.

We've all met the person who goes around offending people by blurting out the first thing that comes to mind. That type of person loves to say: "That's just how I am!" That's just how he or she has *learned* to be.

Often I find that people resist relearning communication because they want to be spontaneous. If your "spontaneous" actions are the result of learning and if these actions are ineffective, what is so wonderful about spontaneity?

Of course, it would be unreasonable to expect you to analyze every word before you utter it. Instead, focus on particular difficulties with particular people: "We always end up fighting." "He never understands what I want." "I lost my head again." Decide to better these ineffective situations by thinking before you speak. We'll be looking at more specific techniques and approaches in the next chapter.

Choose Your Medium

In the past, many companies used to terminate employees by putting a note in their pay envelope—thus the term "to get a pink slip." Imagine how the shock of being told you were fired would be compounded by the impersonality of that method.

An assistant usually has at her disposal at least three methods of communication: face to face, telephone, and written. Which to choose in any situation depends on a number of factors:

1. How much time do you have? In general, the telephone is the quickest.
2. Is there emotional content to this communication, as in a confrontation over some issue? Do you want to see the other person's reaction to some of your ideas? Face to face is best.
3. Do you want a record of this communication? Whenever you want proof of what has been said or are using this communication partly for your own visibility, written communication is best.

Of course, you may have to balance one against the other. For example, you don't always have the time to pursue an issue face to face, even if that method would be ideal. As with any of the other guidelines we're talking about, take time here to look at your communication problems and see if the choice of medium is contributing to the problem anywhere.

Choose Your Words

Not too long ago, I asked those attending one of my seminars to fill out a feedback sheet at the end of the seminar. These sheets are very valuable sources of information to me. Occasionally someone won't like my hairdo or height, but usually the feedback is both positive and useful. After this recent seminar, as I read the evaluations, I came across one with this comment: "Why do you use the phrase 'Where I'm coming from'? Why don't you say what you mean?" I had been guilty of using a phrase that could be considered jargon—language limited to a particular field—and because of it I had obviously alienated this seminar attendee.

Sometimes jargon offends others and makes them less willing to listen. Sometimes it causes the communication to be completely misunderstood. You might drive by a place with this designation and not realize it was what you were looking for: Environmental Waste Management Facility. (That's a garbage dump!) If you were a new employee in a lumber company in the West and someone called you a "factory flitch," would you be pleased or insulted? (The latter. It's what is left of the wood after all the useful parts have been taken off.)

Most industries—and often departments—have their own particular jargon. All it is is a shorthand language among people who understand it. But if you use jargon with the uninitiated they may be offended or just not understand you. Most times in situations like these, people will not question the word or phrase; they will just tune you out.

Choice of words is important in another way. The English language is notorious among language students for the ambiguity of its words. One word may mean many things. Try this little exercise. Write down what you think I mean by each of these words: camel, jack, plane, run.

You probably found yourself hesitating a couple of times to wonder "Which does she mean?" A camel can be an animal or a color. A jack can be a car accessory, a card, or a toy. A plane can be in the air or on a carpenter's bench. And run can refer to an election, a fast movement, a batch of products, or a hole in one's stocking.

As our language changes, the dangers of ambiguity become even more pronounced. If someone asks for "bread," do you send him to a bakery or a bank? To have "grass" may not refer to a lawn. And people may be reluctant to go on vacation and admit to having a "gay" old time. People who are good communicators take time to study the language they use, to understand the nuances of meanings of certain words, and to be aware of how imprecise language can be.

To illustrate how careful we must be in communicating, I want to tell a little story on myself. A while ago, during a break in a seminar, one of the attendees came up to me and said she had a little problem. Could I advise her on how to deal with a "touchy" person? So I started to tell her how one must be aware of why that person is touchy and about what and be delicate, and so forth.

As I talked, the woman began to look at me strangely. Seeing that, I stopped and asked her what was wrong. She was embarrassed as she said hesitantly, "Oh, I guess I didn't make myself very clear. By touchy I meant someone who touches you all the time when they're talking." Now I was embarrassed. Later I told the class the story to illustrate the difficulty of ambiguous words. Of course, it was half my responsibility to clarify what she meant by a word that could have more than one meaning—and the joke, or the lesson, was on me.

Don't Play Telephone

Remember that game called "telephone" we used to play at children's parties? One person would whisper something in another person's ear. The second person would whisper what she'd heard in a third person's ear, and so on. Then when the message got to the last person (maybe the tenth or so), she would repeat it out loud. Invariably, it would be completely different. What started as "ten cents a dance" might come out as "pink and purple pants."

Hilarious at a party. But telephone games in the business environment aren't so funny and may be costly in financial or human terms. The more a message is repeated, the more likely it is that misinterpretations will occur each time. This doesn't happen consciously. It is just the result of each person filtering the message through her own experience and perceptions.

Try to cut down the number of people through whom a message is filtered to three or less. If you hear a lot of "But she told me . . ." and "But I thought . . ." kind of talk, you may be filtering your messages too much.

The telephone phenomenon is why, of course, gossip tends to be both exaggerated and destructive. People process the gossip through their own filters and their own imaginations. What comes out at the end may not only be untrue but also extremely damaging to the person discussed. Don't play this game of telephone at all.

Gear Your Communication to the Individual

Have you ever explained a task in one way to one person and in a different way to another and gotten the same good results from both? Then you have experienced individual focusing of communication. I knew one administrative assistant who had been quite successful supervising office clerks in a rather directive way. The clerks tended to be new in the workplace and looked to the assistant for her expertise and experience.

But then she met her Waterloo—an office temp who happened to be working part-time while she put herself through graduate school. Our assistant bombed out completely using her "I know" approach with the temp, who was not only intelligent but also quite experienced in the business world. The assistant would have been more effective communicating with this woman from a standpoint of "We know and let's share it."

This type of gearing to the individual also means considering a lot of little things that can make your communication understood and accepted by your listener. Do you neglect to call a person by name and by the name he wants to be called? Older people, for example, are often offended by instant first names. Do you turn off your audience by the use of slang or even swearing? That way of speaking is common, everyday parlance with some people but extremely offensive to others.

If you want to be listened to, communicate in terms others understand and in ways they can accept.

Check Your Communication

"Did you hear what I think I said?" is what this guideline is all about. As careful as you are when you are sending a message, things can go wrong. So get in the habit of checking out your communication. But be careful how you do it.

If you say to your listeners, "I want to make sure you listened to me. What did I say?" you will probably not get an answer because you have insulted them by implying that they weren't listening. Instead, put the onus on yourself: "I want to make sure I covered everything. What's your understanding of what I want to do?" Here you are creating an atmosphere in which you encourage other people to be open with you and you know your message has been received. Most people will not admit they didn't understand something. Checking back on your communication will help to clear up any misunderstanding without offending them.

LISTENING

The Quality of Listening

A lot of people look on listening as something they can do while doing something else. The husband "listens" to his wife as he reads the paper. The manager "listens" to his subordinate while he does paperwork. The assistant "listens" to her co-worker as she files. This kind of listening is relatively harmless but, even in these instances, information may be missed and bad feelings engendered by the poor listening.

To try out your own listening ability, get a friend and do this exercise. Each of you will take turns talking, but before one of you can express her ideas to the other, she must first tell the other what she said. For example:

You: I like artichokes.

Other: You said you like artichokes. As far as I'm concerned, I can do without them. But I'm crazy about anything cooked in lemon sauce. Did you ever try chicken in lemon sauce?

You: You said you don't like artichokes but you really like foods cooked in lemon sauce. To answer your question, I've never had chicken in lemon sauce. Isn't it sweet? I'd hate that.

Other: You've never had chicken in lemon sauce and you think it might be too sweet. You don't seem to like foods that are too sweet.

You: No, I didn't mean I don't like sweets. I meant I don't like main dishes that are too sweet.

Other: You don't like main dishes that are too sweet. To answer your question, this dish is quite tart and delicious. . . .

Do this back and forth on any subject you want for about five minutes. When you've finished, come back to the book, and I'll help you analyze your listening ability.

Analyzing Your Listening

How easy was it to tell someone what he or she said? Probably not too easy. And did you find yourself wanting to interrupt or thinking about what *you* wanted to say? Probably yes. Did you experience frustration at how someone else didn't always understand what you meant? I bet you did.

Listening is not only an important communication skill; it is also a difficult one. But listening is important in your job every time you receive an assignment, every time you interview a prospective office member, every time you're thinking of motivating your subordinates. I've designed an acronym to help you to listen better. The acronym is LISTEN. Let's look at what each of the six letters stands for.

Let Yourself Listen

Get out of the habit of viewing listening as a secondary activity. When you're listening, do only that and concentrate on what you hear. Unless you're willing to invest this kind of energy in the listening side of communication, you'll never be good at it.

Ignore Ego Talk

Most of the time when one person listens to another, a monologue goes on inside the listener's head: "I like that. I don't like that. As soon as she stops, I want to say this. Where am I going when I'm finished here? I like that nice picture on the wall. . . ." Notice that all of the sentences contain an "I." When you listen in terms of "I" or ego talk, you tend to filter the words through your own likes and dislikes rather than listen to what the other person is trying to convey. You may even "tune out" if you don't like it.

Another important aspect of ego talk to watch for is the tendency to let emotions take over during the listening process. Let's say, for example, that you are interviewing a prospective new employee. As you listen to her talk about what she did in her last job, you feel a growing dislike for this person. In fact, you don't want to listen to her. At this moment, you must ask yourself why.

The answer might be that you're hearing something about her conduct in her last job that suggests she would not be a good employee. If that is so, it is relevant. But often, in such a situation, if you ask yourself "Why do I dislike this person?" you may find an answer such as "Where did she get the hairdo?" If the hairdo is purely a matter of personal taste and appearance is not important to the job, you can "tell yourself" to concentrate even harder and disregard your personal feelings. This willingness to look at the source of your feelings about others and handle them will enable you to be fair in your communications—and more effective.

In some situations it may be extremely difficult for you to handle your ego talk emotions. What if, for example, you meet someone at a cocktail party and you start talking about what each of you does and about business in general? He then says to you, "Well, I feel that if a woman wants to get ahead in business, she has to be a bitch." That word is like a red flag in front of a bull to a lot of women.

In a case like that, when the emotional content is very strong, I suggest you bring it out into the open. It's one of the few times I recommend interrupting. But do it in a noncritical way. "Could you explain what you mean by that word? It means a lot of different things to different people." In this way, if the speaker wants to have a real discussion, you're off to a good start. If he wants to get a rise out of you, you didn't bite.

We've seen how pervasive ego talk can be while listening. Unless we work at it, most of us will tend to listen in terms of what we like or don't like or our own emotional responses. What can we substitute for that type of listening? That's the next guideline.

Summarize; Analyze

As you listen to another person, what you can be doing instead of indulging in "I" talk is to relate constantly to what the other person is saying. Let's contrast ego talk listening ("I" listening) and "you" listening to see the difference. For example, I am listening to you talk about your recent vacation.

"I" Listening (inside my head): Oh, you went to Puerto Rico. I went there, too. I wonder if you stayed in the same hotel. Oh, I just loved the beach. Oh, yes, that's a good restaurant, but I know a better one. I must tell you about that. I'm getting bored. Let me tell you about my vacation.

"You" Listening (inside my head): Oh, you went to Puerto Rico. You seem very happy about it. You stayed at the Rio Plata Hotel, which you thought was great except you couldn't get a room facing the beach. You especially enjoyed the seafood and you even tried conch, which you had never had before. You seem proud of your "adventurousness" with the food.

See the difference? With "you" listening you will be able to get much more of what the person is saying.

Tune Out Distractions

If you are in a certain kind of listening situation—in a counseling interview, for example—you will probably engineer the environment to provide a better listening opportunity for yourself. You will probably go off with this person to someplace quiet where you won't be disturbed. But we can't always have that luxury while listening to another person. That means we have to work at "tuning out" the distractions. Can you do that? I'll prove you can.

Many of you have had an experience like this. You are sitting in a restaurant having a conversation with another person who is extremely interesting—so interesting, in fact, that you are listening intently. A waiter comes over to the table and says, "Excuse me, do you find the music too loud?" "Music," you say, "what music?" You had not even heard it! That kind of intense listening is unconscious. It comes from the interest you may have in the speaker. Well, if you can do it unconsciously, you can do it consciously. What it takes, primarily, is a willingness to focus in on what the other person is saying.

Encourage with Your Body

That sounds almost suggestive. What I mean, of course, is that in many situations when you are listening to another person, you want to communicate your interest to the other person. That is very complimentary to the speaker, and, often, very practical. If you are counseling an employee, for example, or doing an appraisal interview or a selection interview, you want to encourage the other person to talk so you can get information or clues to behavior. Some of the ways you can use your body to encourage the other to speak are:

Looking at the other person
Nodding your head occasionally
Leaning forward slightly
Raising your eyebrows to show interest

This type of listening is not only an important business skill, it is also a skill we often use in social situations, and it is seen by the speaker as a signal to keep on talking.

Note the Speaker's Body Language

There's an old song with a line that goes: "Your lips tell me no-no, but there's yes-yes in your eyes." The person who wrote that song was an astute observer of the importance of body language.

Often as we listen to another person, we may get certain "impressions." "She's lying." "He doesn't believe what he's saying." "She's unsure." "He'd rather be somewhere else." We get these impressions not through any occult means, but through unconscious observation of many signals that the other person's body is sending out. If we are able to bring these signals to a conscious level, we will be better receivers of the full communication. Generally, after all, it is more difficult for a person to control the body than the words, so the body may be telling us things the speaker is unwilling or unable to say. Here are some common body signs and what they often mean:

Hesitation. A person may be searching for words or could be unsure of what he or she is saying.

Slight smile on face. May indicate either friendliness or lack of belief in what one is saying. Some women wear a constant smile as a way of being ingratiating.

Pointing index finger. Very aggressive behavior. Be aware that the finger alone can make a listener feel defensive.

Rubbing the nose. Often suggests the speaker doubts his own words.

Averting eyes. May indicate shyness or lack of truthfulness.

Folded arms. A classic posture indicating that the person is keeping you out of her sphere. You've got to be careful with this, though. Some people habitually fold their arms for comfort; others when they are cold. You must see the gesture in context.

As you can see from the above, body signals may mean different things. But put in totality, they often give you a message that will contradict a person's words. Do you accuse the person of being a liar? Of course not, but if you do have any doubt, it would be useful to encourage the other person to keep talking on the subject. That way you can figure out more fully what your doubts are and whether there is any basis for them.

To see how this works, let's look in on an administrative assistant who is asking a typist to work on a special report.

A.A.: Jane, Mr. Brown is going to need this report sooner than we had expected. I'd like you to get to it as soon as possible.

T.: Sure, Barbara (sigh) just put it on the pile.

A.A.: I know you get very busy sometimes, Jane. When do you think you'll be able to start this?

T.: (Sarcastic tone) How about next Tuesday?

A.A.: (Laughing.) Is it that bad? Let's see how I can help you sort out your priorities. What are you working on now?

T.: The monthly progress report. I was told that was the most important thing this week.

A.A.: Yes, I can see why you feel pulled in two directions. Leave that to do this one. I think I can get Karen to do parts of the monthly report. You're good at numbers and I want you to work on this report.

By being aware of the unspoken message that the typist was sending with her tone of voice and sighing, the assistant was able to get at the doubts the typist had and resolve them. She also avoided having the typist feel that work was being unfairly dumped on her. Often people will not say what they really think.

Once you start listening to a person's tone and body in addition to his verbal message, you will find almost a whole new world of communication opening up for you. It forestalls a lot of problems, too, that arise from the assumption that people always mean what they say or say what they mean.

In the next chapter, on special kinds of communication, we will be looking at an extension of the basic listening skills. There are techniques of listening you can use to increase your skills as a receiver of communications. At this point, though, promise yourself that you're going to work on your listening habits. Listening is a way of stroking other people, a source of information for you, and a technique that can help you to become more effective in the difficult world of interpersonal relations.

WRITTEN COMMUNICATION

Written communication is one of those areas that evokes an unpleasant reaction in a lot of people. Maybe they have a picture in their minds of a strict English teacher who is about to teach them vague, uninteresting rules about writing. But learning to write better doesn't have to be dull, and it is an important skill for you to learn. The administrative assistant is often responsible for a great deal of her manager's correspondence; she may also be asked to compile and write reports on special problems. Learning to write well is something you want to do. How can you make it more palatable?

I'm going to show you an example of a letter. I'd like you to read it and decide what is ineffective about it. You will probably find more than one thing wrong with it.

Dear Mr. Evans:

We are replying to your letter of the 15th. It is always a pleasure to hear from our customers and to know that we are performing a service for them. Many customers do not take the time to write and this is a shame, for then it is difficult to keep open communications with them and know what they are looking for from us.

As per your request we are afraid we cannot send you a copy of the recent report we compiled on the effectiveness of annealing procedures in cases of systematization and refinement of our copper-coated winches that we completed last year.

We have had some bad experiences with customers who use the report to modify their own winches and we lost business because of it. We have to protect our business; I'm sure you'll agree.

If there is anything else we can do for you, just let us know and we'll be happy to do what we can.

What *isn't* wrong with the letter? The easiest way to critique it is to take it from the standpoint of guidelines against which you can measure any of your own writing. These four guidelines are:

Completeness
Conciseness
Clarity
Consideration

To be complete, in the sense of this guideline, a letter not only has to express all it wants to; it also has to come to the point early. The letter we are using as an example rambles through a whole meaningless paragraph before it says anything substantial. By this time your reader may be so frustrated that he is not in a receptive mood for the rest of the letter. Take time in writing to outline key points first. Then, in the actual writing, get to the point quickly and succinctly.

The greatest problem in organization communication today is related to the second guideline: conciseness. Here I'm referring to the length of sentences and the length of words and phrases. The sentence in paragraph 2 of the letter is 40 words long. The reader probably doesn't know what the subject of the sentence is by the time he gets to the end. People don't have time to decipher such writing. The letter is also "heavy" and old-fashioned because of the use of worn-out phrases like "as per your request."

To improve yourself in the areas of this guideline, aim for sentences no more than 20 words long. Why? Because it makes for a crisp-reading letter that encourages the reader to read it. Also, beware of the tendency that most organization members have to lay on the long words. Many of us, in an effort to impress, use the biggest words we can think of. That may impress, but it doesn't communicate. If your listener doesn't understand, he will probably ignore.

To understand the importance of the third guideline, look at the second paragraph again. What was completed last year—the report or the annealing procedures? You don't know—and may not care.

Your reader has no time to pick through a sentence and try to figure out what it wants to say. That's why clarity is important. To improve in this guideline area, read over your written communications periodically before they go out. Check especially for misleading or unclear items. The basis for grammar and other rules of writing is to make sure that the writing is clear.

If your written communications tend to be misunderstood, you may want to do some finer study of the language and its framework. Sometimes it is helpful to enlist the help of an associate in picking out areas of muddiness in your writing. Have the other person read a sample of your writing and then ask her what she would do as a result of it. You may be surprised.

Consideration, the fourth guideline, means having a clear focus in written communication on the reader, not the writer. In writing, you have a problem you don't have in verbal communication: You are not there when the receiver gets the communication and cannot know if he will choose to read it. You have to motivate the reader in your writing.

In our bad-letter example, the letter was clearly concerned only with the problems of the company that was sending it. In the third paragraph, for example, the tone was almost insulting in its implication that customers could not be trusted. There are two methods I can suggest for you to get the right focus in your writing:

1. In general, put yourself in the role of the reader. How would you feel if you received that letter or memo? Some letters are like a

slap in the face; others make the reader not only want to read the letter, but also feel generally good besides.

2. Specifically, increase the use of the words "you" and "your" in the letter as opposed to "I," "we," and "us." The use of "you" tells the reader that you are talking about him. He then feels part of the letter. Be especially careful with the first word of each paragraph, because this word stands out from the page. The reader would rather see "you" than "I" there.

Now that we have looked at the four guidelines to better written communication and applied them to the sample letter, I'm going to give you a chance to apply your learning. Rewrite the original letter to conform to the four guidelines. Don't read further until you do this. You may want to compare your letter with an improved sample:

> Dear Mr. Evans:
>
> Thank you for your letter. We are always happy to hear from a valued customer.
>
> Unfortunately, we are unable to send you a copy of our annealing report; we have a company policy on keeping such documents internal. Of course, you must have a good reason for asking for it. So I have arranged to have one of our service reps call on you to answer any questions you may have. He will be able to tell you how the annealing process can be of use to your company.
>
> Jack Suiter will be calling you in the next week to arrange an appointment. He will come only at your convenience.
>
> You are an important customer to us, Mr. Evans. We look forward to providing you with the service you need to use our product.

Written communication is a skill that you can take years and a great deal of work to learn. You can also learn to be a better writer more simply on your own. To do so, follow this easy program:

1. In the next ten letters you write, take some extra time to plan the letter, check the meaning, find the average number of words per sentence, and aim your letter at the reader.
2. After those first ten letters, use the process with every tenth letter you write.

3. Once a month, take all the correspondence you have received in one day and divide it into two piles: effective and ineffective. Don't stop to ask why as you sort them; just make an overall judgment. Then go through each pile and analyze why each letter or memo is in that pile. The ineffective communications will tend to be long-winded, full of buzz words, unclear, and sometimes insulting. The effective written communications are short, to the point, clear, and a pleasure to read. This periodic analysis will strengthen the use of the guidelines in your own writing.

In this chapter on basic communications, we have laid the groundwork for your improved communication when speaking, when listening, and when writing. In the next chapter, we will be looking at some specialized techniques for making you more effective.

7

SPECIAL COMMUNICATION TECHNIQUES

or "I'd like to talk to you about. . . ."

In the last chapter on communications, we looked at the basics of speaking, listening, and writing. In this chapter we'll talk more about specific techniques for specific situations. The two major types of communication I'll be exploring with you are assertiveness and active listening.

ASSERTIVENESS

As in the area of time management, there are certain myths about assertive communication that may serve as barriers to your learning and using the technique. Let's look at these barriers:

Barrier 1. You Are or You Aren't (Assertive).

This is part of the "I am what I am" school. If you're not assertive you never will be. In Chapter 1 we spent a good deal of time examining the basis of male and female behavior and established the fact that all of us tend to behave the way we have learned to behave. It's the same with communication. You have learned to communicate in a certain way and, if you now find it ineffective, you can learn a new way—assertiveness.

Barrier 2. Assertiveness Makes You a "Heavy."

When asked to picture an assertive woman, too many people see a strident female marching with a placard and yelling slogans. If you believe that, of course you don't want to be more assertive. But that image is false. The assertive woman is able to express her ideas, but she is also able to listen, to care for others' feelings, and to make others feel comfortable around her.

Barrier 3. Assertiveness Is Difficult to Learn.

It's not the learning that is difficult; it's the doing. That is why in this chapter I'll give you some practice in assertiveness to make using the techniques easier for you.

Barrier 4. Assertiveness Gets You What You Want.

Nothing gets you what you want. Assertiveness is a very useful technique that can increase your effectiveness enormously. It isn't a 100 percent guarantee. But wouldn't you rather be 80 percent effective than 30 percent?

You've seen what assertiveness is not. Now let's see what it is. Consider assertiveness a golden mean between two less effective extremes. For example, imagine this situation: You have been working late a couple of times a week for the last month to finish a special project. Today you are feeling good about getting all your work done and are looking forward to going to dinner and the movies tonight with a friend. At 4:30 P.M. your manager comes to you and says, "I'm going to have to ask you to work tonight to finish these budget calculations for tomorrow morning's meeting.

At this moment you have before you at least three choices of behavior. You can sigh and settle in for a long and frustrating evening. In that case your manager will be relatively happy but you will not.

A second choice is to take all the rage and frustration that has been building in you during these weeks of overtime and say to your boss: "How could you expect me to work one more night? You're—you're inconsiderate!" With this choice you have aggressed against the other person. Aside from hurting his feelings, you may have put yourself in a very bad position vis-à-vis your job.

A third choice would be a problem-solving appraoch: "It will be very difficult for me to work tonight, as I've made plans for the evening. Is there any other way this can be handled?" Possible alternatives might be:

Have someone else do the job, at least in part
Prepare a skeleton
Come in early the next morning
Have the manager do it

You *may* end up staying and doing it as the manager asked, but you have increased the odds that you won't. Even if circumstances seem to determine that you must stay, you will feel better in that you explored other possibilities instead of accepting and hating it.

Three Choices

The three choices in the little story were based on the three choices you have in any communication situation: nonassertiveness, assertiveness, and aggression. Let's clarify these terms.

Nonassertiveness is a denial of one's rights. People who are nonassertive tend to have difficulty expressing their ideas and feelings and often have a low self-image as a result. The nonassertive person may become a martyr. Remember Marian the Marshmallow in Chapter 3? All U and no I.

Assertiveness is acceptance of all people's rights, mine and others. People who are assertive can say what they think, but are also good at listening and are aware of other people's feelings. The assertive person uses communication to further her own ends without intentionally thwarting others. It is a balance of concern for U and I.

Aggressiveness is a domination of others through a sole concern for one's own rights. The aggressive person expresses her ideas but cares little for their effect on others. Tessie the Tank, the aggressive woman, rolls over everyone in sight. An example of all I but no U.

Now I'd like you to check your understanding of these concepts. Imagine that you are assistant to the manager of administrative services. You have worked for him for three years and all along you were given to believe that you were being groomed for his position. The announcement of his pending promotion has just come through and, as you are called into his office, you expect to be told the job is yours. Instead he says, "Brenda, you've worked with me for three years and have done a fantastic job. No one knows the department as well as you do. For that reason I'm going to put you in charge of training my replacement. He starts tomorrow."

Before you read on, take a minute out and write what you think would be a nonassertive, an assertive, and an aggressive response. There are a number of possibilities for each one. Here are some suggestions to compare with yours.

Nonassertive: (Gulp.) "What exactly do you want me to do?"

Aggressive: "You mean to tell me that after all these years you're going to bring in somebody else? You must be crazy if you think I'm going to help you!"

Assertive: "I'm honestly dumbfounded, Mac. I was always told that I was to be your replacement. We'd better talk about this."

I think it's obvious why the nonassertive response is ineffective. You will never get what you want with it. The difficulties of the aggressive position are somewhat less obvious. You're angry, after all, and rightly so. Why not say it? Because you're accusing the other person and that doesn't put him in a position in which he's willing to talk it over with you. If I am being beaten over the head, I would be justified in being aggressive toward my attacker, but in most business situations "going for the jugular" should not be considered a primary response.

The merits of the assertive response are, first of all, that it permits you to say what you feel. That can be an emotional release. It also opens discussion with the other party. You may or may not get the promotion, but at least you may be able to get support for another move that would be useful in your career. You could even choose to quit and go elsewhere, but you are still richer because you have expressed your feelings and your rights. (I'm impelled to say here that under the right circumstances you might move into an aggressive mode, especially if you have any documentation and other power backing. It depends. But there is nothing worse than trying to use aggressiveness when you have nothing to back you up.)

If you think back to the ideas we talked about in Chapter 1 on the woman in business, you will realize that our society's rearing process tends to push men and women into two different slots in terms of the assertiveness model. Men tend to be trained to veer to the aggressive side (independent, loud, commanding) and women are encouraged to be nonassertive (gentle, quiet, nice). Bringing such programming into your adult life, you may be responding constantly to inner messages that say "Be nice," "Don't be angry," "You shouldn't be forward," "Nice girls don't fight."

Of course some men are nonassertive, some women are aggressive, and many of both are sometimes assertive. You have to look at your own behavior—and you'll get a chance to do that in this chapter—to determine what your problems are.

Incidentally, it may help you to know that there are very few purely assertive people. Most people have specialized assertiveness problems. These problems can be classified by different environments, different people, and different situations. I'm going to help you appraise your own difficulties through the use of my assertiveness scales.

Test Your Own Assertiveness

Scale 1: Environments

On the following scale, place a W at the place that describes what you consider to be your normal communication mode at work. Place an H to indicate your normal communication behavior at home.

Nonassertive — Assertive — Aggressive

Very often people act quite differently in these two situations. A woman may be very assertive at work, for example, but be at the mercy of her children at home. A woman could be nonassertive at work and yet assertively manage her outside life. Although this book is written to increase your effectiveness at the office, your overall self-confidence will be enhanced if you can work out communication improvement in many facets of your life.

Scale 2: People

Write down the names of three people at work with whom you have difficulty communicating. It may be a case where you end up in continuous arguments. You may end up with bad feelings. You may not be able to achieve what you want with this person. Whatever the difficulty, beside each name place an I at the point on the scale that you think describes your usual behavior toward that person.

Person 1 ______________________________

Nonassertive	Assertive	Aggressive

Person 2 ______________________________

Nonassertive	Assertive	Aggressive

Person 3 ______________________________

Nonassertive	Assertive	Aggressive

Do you see a trend in your behavior toward one side or the other? Do you tend to be too nonassertive with some people and too aggressive with others? The administrative assistant may have a mixed problem. Most people, women particularly, find it a problem to be assertive enough with those in authority, like their boss. In combination with this, and sometimes as a result of it, the same person may be too aggressive with juniors. It's almost as if we can only take so much passivity. It builds up and we have to take it out on someone else. The "kick the cat" syndrome—coming home and lashing out at the first thing or person you see—is part of the same phenomenon.

Scale 3: Situations

For each of the following five situations, place an I on the scale to indicate your work behavior.

Asking for something

I tend to do things myself	I can ask for what I need	I ask without giving and may even demand

Saying no

I say yes even when I shouldn't	When it is required I can say no to a request	I say no too often and in a heavy manner

Expressing feelings and opinions

I am not comfortable saying what I think and feel	I feel comfortable telling others what I think and feel	I put the responsibility for my feelings on others and never elicit their opinions

Giving criticism

I don't like to give negative feedback at all	I can give negative feedback when called for	I tend to make others feel bad when I criticize

Receiving criticism

I tend to get defensive in the face of criticism	I can accept valid criticism and learn from it	I tend to turn the criticism around and attack others

Most people have some perception of their own problems. That's why self-evaluation like that on the previous scales can be useful. But sometimes we fool ourselves. To make this analysis even more useful, I suggest you do it on yourself and then do it with a friend. Each of you decide where the other will lie on the scales. You will get a much fuller picture of your behavior.

Now let's talk about each of these areas to define the problem further. Then we'll go on to techniques.

Asking for something. This is a common assertiveness difficulty. I have seen, for example, a group of women sit in a seminar room hugging themselves because it was chilly. But no one would ask if the heat could be turned up. That is the nonassertive way of dealing with it. The assistant who has this difficulty may try to do too much at work and not ask for help from others. Just as ineffective, of course, is the person who demands of others. She may be like the assistant I knew who had the habit of throwing papers on people's desks and telling them to "get these out." Assertively asking for something means stating what you want in a manner that is acceptable and even pleasant for the other person.

Saying no. How many office collections have you contributed to without really wanting to? If the answer is many, you may be on the nonassertive side of this situation. The aggressive way of dealing with a request would be to say no without regard to other's needs, the "No, I won't help you at all" answer. As in so many other types of behavior, the key to effectiveness is balance—being able to say no when appropriate and sometimes agreeing to things that will benefit both you and others.

Expressing feelings and opinions. Nonassertive people spend a lot of time ruminating over things that have happened: "I should have told him. . . ." "I hope she knows how angry I am." "I bet that look I gave her made her think twice." "If only I had thought to say to him. . . ." All of these are ineffective because hoping that others know how we feel isn't any guarantee that they do. We have to tell them. Women may be relatively comfortable talking about "sad" feelings; it's angry feelings that are the usual problem. Some nonassertive women will smile and accept behavior when they are really offended by it. Why? Because they don't want to make a fuss. Unfortunately, that lack of expression tends to build up in emotional energy and can come out in slamming doors, yelling at innocent bystanders, and getting knots in the stomach and headaches. Sometimes it comes out as the opposite of what she feels—tears. (Since it's "okay" for a woman to cry, she may do so even when she's angry.)

The aggressive person will express her feelings but will put the blame on others: "You make me feel bad when you do that." The assertive person is willing to express her feelings but would put it differently: "I get angry when that happens." The assertive administrative assistant will want to state her opinions, let someone know if she is unhappy about something, and be willing to ask for the kind of treatment she wants.

Giving criticism. If you got a sloppily typed letter from a typist, what would you say to her? You might grumble and go fix it up yourself. That would be nonassertive. You might say "This is the worst example of typing I've ever seen. You should be ashamed of yourself." That would be aggressive. You could also say "I don't think this letter is up to our standards. What do you think?" That is an example of assertive communication. The real "trick" in criticism is being objective ("our standard") and being open to the other person ("What do you think?").

Receiving criticism. People who are nonassertive hate to receive criticism because it makes their already low self-image sink further. Surprisingly, the most assertive way to be criticized (for a valid criticism) is to admit it: "I did forget to send that out. How can I get the information to them quickly?" The worst thing you can do is to make excuses: "It was a bad day." "We are so busy." "No one helped me." "You gave me so much to do." The more excuses you give, the more defensive you appear, and defensiveness is a very nonassertive behavior. On the other hand, the "you should talk" type of reaction to criticism is very aggressive. It turns the attack in the other direction, but it usually results in a fight.

You've taken some time to look over your individual assertiveness problems. To capsule these exercises for your use, fill in the answers to the following statements:

1. My chief difficulty at work is that I tend to be too ____________.
2. I have assertiveness problems with ____________________ kind of people, for example, with ______________________________.
   (name)
3. Two situations in which I would like to be more assertive are ______________________________ and ______________________________.

Techniques

Like any other communication model, assertiveness has special techniques you can use to make it easier to follow the model. I'm going to describe some of these techniques, give examples of where you can use them, and then have you do some practice exercises to apply your new knowledge.

Assertiveness Technique No. 1. I-Talk

When we talked in Chapter 3 about the possible combinations of U and I in interpersonal relations, we referred to the all-U person as a marshmallow. If you have ever known a marshmallow, you know that this person doesn't know what I-talk is.

To be credible and demand respect, a person must be able to express her own ideas and opinions. I-talk is the chief technique with which to do that. To use this technique, you use the word "I": "I want. . . ." "I don't want. . . ." "I prefer. . . ." "I'd like to talk to you. . . ." "I'm not happy with what is happening."

This approach may seem quite egotistic to you, but remember that assertiveness is a balance and there will be other techniques, such as listening, to provide that balance. To a person who uses I-talk automatically, it may not seem like a technique at all. But if you don't use it and start doing so, you will find an enormous difference in the way people treat you.

I-talk is useful to demand respect through your expertise: "I think we ought to go ahead on this project." It also permits you to express without aggressing against another person. There is a great deal of difference between an aggressive: "You have no right to talk to me like that," and an assertive: "I'm not comfortable with the way you're talking."

Assertiveness Technique No. 2. Broken Record

One of the most common manifestations of nonassertiveness is the inability to say no. Most people who have this difficulty end up saying yes because they do not persist. Broken record will help you to keep your point of view.

To use this technique, when another person asks you to do something you don't want to do, adopt one phrase and keep repeating it. Let's look at an example. There is a character you will find in many companies. She may be an assistant or secretary like you. Unlike you, she tends to let her work slide; then she comes to you asking for help. This is not a person who really needs help; this is someone who has been taking advantage of you. You want to stop it, but you don't want to be too aggressive, because you have to work with this person.

Here she comes, with that usual "I don't know where the time goes" look on her face.

Miss Manipulative: "Could you help me? I got behind and I'll never finish this special report the vice-president wants."

The Assertive Assistant: "I won't be able to help you with your work today."

Miss Manipulative: "But why? I'm sure you have a *little* time."

The Assertive Assistant: "I won't be able to help you with your work today."

Miss Manipulative: "Oh come on, be a friend. I'll be in trouble if I don't get this done."

The Assertive Assistant: "I hear you, but I won't be able to help you with your work today."

Miss Manipulative: "But you're so fast and clever; it won't take you any time."

The Assertive Assistant: "I won't be able to help you with your work today."

Nowhere in this dialog have you offended the other person. All you did was maintain your position. Why is it so important to keep to one phrase? Because if you try to answer her manipulative ploys ("Why?" "Be a friend." "You're so clever."), she will be able to out-argue you into a yes.

The broken record technique is useful whenever you want to maintain your position:

> "You did promise me a raise in six months."
> "We did agree it would be ready on Friday."
> "I won't be able to complete that in three hours."
> "We're not interested in buying a new typewriter."

Assertiveness Technique No. 3. Turnaround

This is a technique I've developed myself. And it's very useful for women in business because many women have to deal with put-downs. Exactly what is a putdown, you ask. My experience has been that it varies with the individual. Men may see women as overly sensitive to what they consider innocent remarks or even compliments. ("You're looking lovely today" is not the best way to greet a woman at a business meeting.) Even women may disagree on what is or is not a putdown. (Does "sweetheart" or "honey" drive *you* up the wall?) Often the putdown is more by implication than by a direct insult, and that makes it more difficult to deal with.

For example, a manager starts a meeting with "It's nice to have you ladies here today." He probably doesn't mean anything negative but, by calling attention to the fact that the presence of women is an unusual occurrence, he may make the women seem like outsiders. If you are one of the women, you could ignore it, but that might affect your credibility at the meeting. You could say something like "What do you mean by that?" but the man speaking—and the other men in the room—will think you're crazy to ask about something they see as a compliment. So use the turnaround: "Thank you. I'm sure we can bring something unique to the meeting." You've effectively turned the fact that you are different from a negative point to a positive one.

Let me give you another example, because this technique needs more expertise than many of the others. You have just come out of a department meeting where you were involved with your boss—a vice-president—and a group of managers—his subordinates—in discussing the possibilities of bringing a job enrichment program to your area of the company. You took a strong stand for the proposed idea, basing your opinion on the importance of managing human resources most effectively. As you leave the meeting, one of the managers says to you sarcastically: "You women are really hung up on people, aren't you?" Using the turnaround, you could answer, "Yes, and a concern for people is really a mark of a good manager these days, isn't it?"

The key to the turnaround is taking an implied insult and turning it into a self-compliment. It's a technique that requires practice, but it will reward you by making you feel better about yourself and increasing your "image."

Other Assertiveness Techniques

The techniques we have talked about up to now are used mainly to enhance the person herself, to take her away from nonassertiveness. But there is the danger of going too far. Imagine what the world would be like if all people did was ask for what they wanted, say no all the time, and turn everything to their own advantage: Horrible. That's why there are other techniques in the assertiveness model to balance the egotistic concerns. We have talked about two of these techniques already in the book: stroking and listening.

The kind of stroking we are talking about here, of course, is positive stroking, giving positive recognition to another person. It is useful in making the other person feel less defensive and therefore more open to you: "I know you have made this department successful on the basis of similar approaches, but I'd like you to look at some new options that could be just as useful." "Thank you for considering me but I won't be able to sit on that committee." "You have a right to be upset about this mistake but I am uncomfortable when you yell like that."

Use stroking, but use it judiciously. Someone recently said to me after I had explained the use of stroking, "Oh, that's what it is. In our company you always know when someone's been away at a seminar because he comes back and praises everyone to the skies. It's ridiculous." Done that way it *is* ridiculous, but the basic technique isn't. Don't use stroking so often and so indiscriminately (everyone's tie or dress is beautiful) that you become manipulative and artificial. Use it honestly. If you hate someone's hair don't tell her it's beautiful just so you can get something you want. That is not only irresponsibly manipulative, it is also stupid. Many people know when someone else is telling the truth or not by intuitively reading them. If you are not, you will be seen in a very negative way.

In Chapter 6 we talked about listening as a technique. Listening to the other person's point of view is the perfect balance to I talk: "I have doubts about this approach. What do you think?" "I'm unhappy with the way we've been getting along lately. How do you feel about it?" "I won't be able to work overtime this week. How can we arrange the work to get it all done?"

There is an extension of listening called active listening that deserves a section of its own. It is a technique that is invaluable to the administrative assistant in any kind of interview situation: selection, appraisal, counseling. I'll explain active listening to you later in the chapter. First, take some time out to practice your new assertiveness techniques. For each of the following situations, think up a phrase you could use to be assertively effective:

Assertiveness Practice

1. You and Jane are both assistants to executives. After you get your new car, Jane asks you if you can give her a ride home every night on a regular basis. You feel it would be inconvenient. You answer:

   ____

   ____

2. For the past two years, you've organized the City Charity drive for your company. Your manager wants you to handle it again this year. You don't want to. You say:

   ____

   ____

3. A male employee from another department calls you "honey" constantly. It is driving you crazy. You want him to stop but want to keep on good terms with him. You say:

 ____

 ____

4. A department typist is coming in late periodically. Your manager asks you to speak to her. You approach her and say:

 ____

 ____

5. Your boss has just informed you that he has decided not to send you to a professional association meeting in another city. A few months ago he had promised to send you and you think going would be important to your career growth. You say:

 ____

 ____

There is no one right answer for any of these. There is a range of assertive replies, the choice of which depends on your own style. I'll give you some suggestions.

1. *Possible Answers*

   "No, I won't be able to."

   "No, I'm sorry, I'd rather not be tied down that way."

   "I can't take you on a regular basis but when I *am* going straight home I'll check to see if you want a ride."

Comments. The first one is most direct. The last one is "softer." You are not obligated to do this, but if you want to it is a very kind thing to do. If you say no and Jane asks why, go into the broken record. "I won't be able to." Once you start trying to explain, your reasons will be countered and you are lost.

2. *Possible Answers*

   "I won't be able to do it this year."

   "Thank you for your confidence, but I won't be able to do it again."

   "Thank you, I won't be able to do it. But I would be willing to give some pointers to the person who does."

Comments. Again the possible answers range from "hard" to "soft," and two of them are further softened with a stroking "Thank you." What you are comfortable with and what you are willing to do determine the best answer for you. Be careful about offering to help if you don't really want to. That's just nonassertiveness all over again.

3. *Possible Answers*

   "Harry, I'd rather you didn't call me honey."

   "Harry, I know you mean well, but I don't feel comfortable being called honey. Please call me by my name."

Comments. Most people continue using words and phrases that are offensive to others because they don't realize how offensive they are. And as long as they don't know, they will continue. The nonassertive person often puts up with unwanted behavior because she doesn't know how to ask someone to stop. In dealing with a problem like this, stay away from "you" phrases and stick with "I." Your listener will tend to be less defensive this way.

4. *Possible Answers*

   "Susan, I'd like to talk to you about your lateness during the last few weeks. What is the problem?"

   "Susan, I'm concerned about your increasing lateness. Let's talk about it."

   "Susan, I've noticed that you've been late three times in the last two weeks. We expect our typists to be here on time. What is happening?"

Comments. A combination of I-talk and listening is the most effective way to handle a situation like this. Whenever you are in the position of criticizing, or seeming to criticize, someone else, as in No. 3 and here, avoid "you" phrases: "You've been late too often lately." "You shouldn't call me that." "You make me mad." State your problem from the "I" standpoint and then balance it off by being willing to listen to the other person's point of view.

5. *Possible Answers*

   "John, I was really counting on going to that meeting. What is the problem?"

   "John, I'm taken aback. That meeting is very important to me. Can we talk about it?"

"John, I'm dumbfounded. I want very much to go to that meeting. Is there any way it can be arranged?"

Comments. Don't try to cover your feelings, but don't let them get out of hand. I-talk is an excellent technique for that. Express how important the meeting is to you. Open discussion. That is the only way you can ultimately get to some solution of the problem. You may get exactly what you want; you may get a compromise; you may get nothing more than the satisfaction of expressing your feelings and opinions. Any of these can be seen as an assertiveness payoff.

Visual Assertiveness

Assertiveness is primarily a verbal communication technique, but we must look at another aspect of communication that is very important to the person trying to be more assertive: body language. We've talked briefly about this aspect of communication in the previous chapter. In assertiveness, as in communication in general, the body communicates as much as or more than the verbal message. If you can learn to monitor and control your body's message, you will be able to reinforce what your words are saying rather than counteract them.

Let's look at the relative types of body language used by a nonassertive, an aggressive, and an assertive person. In a communication situation each would tend to behave in this way:

The nonassertive person

Avoids eye contact with the other person
Holds the head down
Hugs the body when talking, almost as if closing oneself in
Speaks in a low tone of voice, sometimes inaudible

The aggressive person

Looks at people directly, even belligerently
Uses noise-making gestures such as pounding the desk
Points at others when talking to them
Yells
Pushes the body forward almost threateningly

The assertive person

Keeps hands at side, neither aggressively pointing nor nonassertively closing in
Maintains eye contact in an interested manner
Speaks in a well-modulated voice
Listens with nodding head and other facial signs of involvement
Smiles occasionally

One of the first things an actress does to put herself into a role is to align her body to conform to the personality of the character she is playing. If you are working at making yourself more assertive, you must start becoming aware of the body signals you send out. Do these body signs conform to your assertiveness or do they diminish it? Especially when you are about to go into a situation in which you want to act assertively, be aware of aligning your body to conform to your words.

Assertiveness is one of the most useful yet most misunderstood techniques that has come along in the last few years. The businesswoman needs to be assertive to accomplish her aims. This technique can help her to get the respect and even the admiration she would like from others.

ACTIVE LISTENING

A second communication technique is called active listening. In the last chapter we looked at the difficulties of effective listening and how to improve yourself in this communications area. Here, we will go a step further and show you some different kinds of listening and how you can use them to be more effective in your job.

Active listening is a way of extending the listening technique to accomplish special aims in special situations. Active listening can be very important in dealing with the emotions in another person's message. It can be useful in a counseling situation, when you want to help an employee find answers to her problems. It can be a means of improving your rapport with those around you.

Here are some of the active listening techniques you use to extend your effectiveness as a listener.

Silence

This may seem funny to you, but if you think about it, it isn't. How many times a day do you hear two people talking to one another and vying with each other to get the next word in? And they call that conversation. Being willing to silence yourself and let another person talk is one of the most unselfish things you can do; good listeners are always in demand. It is also a very useful thing to keep in mind in an interview; for example, when you ask a question and get no answer. Give it some time. Most of us hate silence and rush in to fill the void. But if you force yourself to wait a few extra seconds, the interviewee will probably start to speak and you will be fulfilling your aim.

Paraphrasing

This is the most common type of active listening, the one you will use most frequently. Essentially, it is summarizing the gist of what the other person said:

"So what you're saying is that you feel you would be able to do a better job if you had more training."
"You want me to do the report the same way I did it last year, but cut it down by about one-third."
"You can probably get the data to me by tomorrow. If you run into any snags you'll call me by 5 today."

In paraphrasing, you are sending back to the speaker what you've received. This serves as a check for you. Is what I heard what was really said? It is also a very positive type of feedback to the individual because it tells that person you have listened well. People will respect you for paying such close attention to them.

Echoing

The word "why" often puts people off. It puts them on the defensive because they feel called on to defend what they've said or done. Echoing of content can often be used in place of "why" and produce much better results. Say, for example, that you are talking to that young typist who has been coming in late. She says to you, "I just can't seem to get up in the morning." You say, "You can't seem to get up in the morning." This reaffirmation of what she said will tend to make her go on and talk about what she feels are the reasons for this. If you asked her why, you might get a shrug of the shoulders—end of conversation.

Echoing is also a very good technique when you are not sure what another person meant and don't want to jump to conclusions. For example, you approach an office temporary with something you want her to do, and she says "I can't do that." This almost sounds like insubordination, and some assistants in that situation would counter with "Oh yes, you can and you will!" Try, instead, echoing: "You can't do that?" You will tend to get a reason: "I don't know how." "I was told to work only until 12." "I just received another assignment." Echoing can help keep you out of possible conflict situations based on a reaction by assumption.

Reflecting Nonverbal Content

You are showing a new employee around on her first day of work. As you introduce her to people and tell her all the things she has to know about hours, washrooms, the cafeteria, and so on, you notice she has this lost look on her face. You remember what it is like to start a new job and to be overcome by all the new faces and information. So you say to her, "It's kind of hard the first day, isn't it?" "It sure is," she sighs, and smiles thankfully. You can almost see the nervousness come out of her like steam through a safety valve. And that's exactly what has happened. By verbalizing her feelings, you have helped her to vent her emotions. Once released in this way, emotions tend to get played out and not be the strong barrier they could be to communication.

This technique can be used with any emotion:

A nervous prospective employee. "Job interviews aren't always easy."
A crying employee. "I can see how upset you are over this."
An angry manager. "Of course you are angry about what happened."
A depressed friend. "It's been terrible for you, hasn't it?"

By helping the other person to vent her emotion, you enable that person to recover much more quickly and get on to whatever realistic steps have to be taken to solve the problem.

Many people can accept using this technique when emotions like sadness are involved, but why should you reinforce an angry person?

Won't that make him angrier? No. Most of us are in the habit of trying to stop unpleasantness such as anger because it is so uncomfortable. So we tell people to stop and not be angry. The trouble is that we might be able to stop the outward manifestations of the anger, such as yelling, but it only gets bottled up and will tend to "leak" out in unpleasant, indirect ways. Better to experience that emotional fury for a short period of time and have it over with. Otherwise it will color that person's actions all day. It's healthier and ultimately more effective for you to be able to express *your* feelings in I-talk; it's just as effective to help others express theirs by reflecting those messages you are receiving nonverbally.

Active Listening Practice

Now for some practice. Use a type of active listening to deal with each of the following situations. What could you say?

1. After a general meeting with your office staff, one of the junior clerks comes to you and says dejectedly, "I thought I made some good points at that meeting, but no one paid any attention to me."

   ____

   ____

2. An employee from another department is pointing out an error your department made. She says complainingly, "You people never do anything right."

   ____

   ____

3. You arrive home late because of traffic and your husband says as you come in the door, "This is the last straw in a horrible day. Now dinner will be late too!"

   ____

   ____

4. A customer yells at you over the phone, "They've pushed me from pillar to post for half an hour. I want some action!"

   ____

   ____

Here are some possible answers for you to compare with yours.

1. *Possible Answers*
   "You felt ignored."
   "You can't understand why your ideas weren't accepted."

Comments. The normal tendency for the listener here is to start giving advice: "Now this is what you should do next time. . . ." There may be a place for advice, but your dejected person isn't ready for that. She has to be helped to get through the emotional barrier she is feeling before she will be ready to talk about solutions.

2. *Possible Answer*
   "We never do anything right?"

Comments. I suggest one approach here—echoing. Most people would be surprised if they could hear themselves talk. All of us tend to speak in exaggerated terms at times, especially under emotional conditions. The speaker here is probably angry over the mistake your department made. She's not choosing her words. By your echoing her statement, she will probably be led to see how outrageous her statement was and will probably return with "Well, I didn't mean *any*thing." Then you can step in and offer to do what is necessary to remedy the situation.

Without clarification by echoing there would probably be an escalation of exaggerated accusations between the two of you. ("Look who's talking. Last month when. . . .") Bad feelings would rise and would tend to affect your future relationships. I'm not suggesting that you be "nice" to people. I'm showing you ways to deal with them as human beings. Eventually you will get a return by the better working relationship you have with them. You will also feel good about yourself because of your improved ability to handle people.

3. *Possible Answers*
   "It must have been a terrible day for you to be so upset."
   "You look terrible!"

Comments. When I use this example in my seminars, there are two other kinds of responses that are suggested most frequently. Let's look at these less effective approaches to uncover the pitfalls.

"*You* had a bad day. Let me tell you about mine."

The difficulty here is that no matter how loving your spouse is, he doesn't care at this moment about your day. He cares about his own.

Selfish? No. *Real*. If you give him some empathy, show him you accept his feelings, he will be more likely to listen to your tale of woe.

"Forget it. Let's go out to dinner."

You might want to come to this after the active listening. But don't jump to it first. Otherwise you may sit through a very unpleasant dinner with your husband quietly ruminating about his day and feeling, in addition, very misunderstood. Unexpressed emotions tend to "hang around" and affect behavior in ways that have nothing to do with the matter at hand.

4. *Possible Answers*

   "I realize how frustrated you feel at the moment. How can I help you?"

   "You certainly haven't gotten the information you need. What is it you're looking for?"

Comments. This is a good example of the practicality of active listening. It doesn't require you to sit for hours and listen. It requires an attitude and acceptance that people in general are much more emotional than we think. In this case your recognition of the person's emotional state will help to calm him down.

Communication between people is not easy. As long as you assume it is, you will not have the motivation to work at improving your communication skills. In this chapter we looked at two techniques: assertiveness and active listening. Both techniques require hard work. But both offer you the payoff of better solutions to problems, better working relationships, and better feelings about yourself.

8

PROBLEM SOLVING AND DECISION MAKING

or "There's only one way to handle this."

Just about anyone in a management or management-related job has many problems to solve and decisions to make over the course of a day. This chapter is a guide on how to deal with them.

PROBLEMS AND DECISIONS

First, let's distinguish between problem solving and decision making. A problem always ends up in a decision. A decision does not have to start with a problem. Let us say, for example, that you have been asked to choose a simple word processing unit for your office. You have to make a decision by finding out what equipment is available and choosing the best one for your purpose. That's the decision-making process.

On the other hand, let's say that you have been asked by your boss to find out why productivity in the office is so low. You start with a general problem—how to increase productivity—that you have to explore and define. Depending on what the real problem is (routine work, paper flow, outdated equipment) you will find alternative ways to deal with that problem. One of the alternatives may be word processing equipment.

As in all other areas of management, your problems and decisions will have to do with either things or people. Some of your problem solving and decision making will be focused on such things as equipment, procedures, work flow, or systems. Probably a majority of your problems and decisions will have to do with people.

MAKING DECISIONS

We're going to explore an approach to decision making first. I'll show you the steps involved and then take you through the process with an example. The decision-making process consists of five steps:

Establish purpose
Set criteria
Develop alternatives
Choose best alternative
Implement that decision

Let's look at an example. Your manager informs you, to your delight, that you are being given a chance to take some formal training to help you in your job. You can decide on how you want to do it. How *do* you decide what kind of formal training is best for you?

Establish Purpose

This step entails putting together a simple statement of what you want to achieve with this decision. The statement of purpose will help to keep you on track during the decision-making process. In this case, your purpose could be stated: "To obtain, within the next six months, the best formal training for my job that I can."

Set Criteria

Once you start looking at alternatives, the amount of information may make handling unwieldy. Therefore, even before you get to alternatives, it's a good idea to decide what standards you will use to measure your possible choices against. Most often, time and money will both be considerations in your decision making. Take a few minutes to write down what criteria you think would be most important in this case. Then compare them with some sample criterias:

Time: Limit of three days maximum away from work; not during spring, which is a very busy time for us

Money: Limit of $X, including expenses
Personal Preferences: Block of training at least two days long
Level: Prefer assistant; might take supervisor
Content: Especially human relations and time management
Quality: Reputable association or school; credible teacher

Develop Alternatives

One of the major pitfalls in decision making comes at this stage. There is a tendency to think of one or two possible solutions and then to make the decision. In general, at this stage, go instead for quantity. Think up as many possible solutions as you can. Don't worry about evaluating them. That will come later. Here you just want to get them down. In the case of our example, alternatives may not come easily to you. You might have to do some research to find out what types of training are available. You could ask other assistants; you could ask people in personnel; you could call schools or associations; you could read newspaper and magazine ads to get your data. Let's assume you have done this and have come up with these alternatives within the next six months.

Night-school ten-week course for supervisors at community college
Two-day university-sponsored course for administrative assistants in April
One-day Professional Secretaries International-sponsored seminar in February
Certification correspondence course for executive secretaries
Three-day public seminar for administrative assistants in June

Choose from Among Alternatives

There are many ways to make a decision or choose from among alternatives. One of the best, when you have a variety of both alternatives and criteria, is to set up a decision matrix like the one shown. Here each alternative is measured against each criterion to determine which alternative best fits all the criteria. To prepare the decision matrix, set up vertical columns with each criterion as a heading. We have chosen Time, Money, Preference, Level, Content, and Quality. Yours may be different. Then write down your alternatives along the side. We have used Night School, 2-day Univ., P.S.I., Correspondence, and 3-Day Public. Again, your choices may be different. Next block off a grid to measure the horizontal against the vertical.

	Time	*Money*	*Preference*	*Level*	*Content*	*Quality*	*Total*
Night School							
2-Day Univ.							
P.S.I.							
Correspondence							
3-Day Public							

To use the matrix, you consider each alternative and ask yourself how it measures up against each criterion. One easy way to evaluate the data is to assign a number to each box: 0 for a poor solution, 1 for a good solution, 2 for an excellent solution. For example, the first alternative is a night-school course. Measure each criterion against this course:

Time: Not a block of time and does extend into the spring, a very busy time for us	1
Money: Well within the budget	2
Preferences: I prefer a block training	0
Level: Supervisory, not assistant	1
Content: Lot of human relations, no time management	1
Quality: Good school, personal recommendation	2
	7

After you have done that for each alternative, your matrix will look something like this:

	Time	*Money*	*Preference*	*Level*	*Content*	*Quality*	*Total*
Night School	1	2	0	1	1	2	7
2-Day Univ.	0	1	2	2	1	1	7
P.S.I.	1	2	1	2	1	2	9
Correspondence	1	1	0	2	2	1	7
3-Day Public	2	1	2	2	2	2	11

According to the analysis, the three-day seminar seems to be the best choice. The one-day seminar is close. In real life either might do and you might make your decision on the basis of convenience or preference. Notice that the strength of the decision matrix depends in great part on choosing the most important criteria. In deciding on a piece of equipment, the criteria would probably be such things as cost, time of installation, servicing, estimated life, and trade-in possibilities. Another important thing to remember in using a decision matrix is to be sure you get the data you need to evaluate each alternative validly.

Implement the Decision

Plan what steps you have to go through to accomplish your purpose. In this example, you want to consider:

Checking the time off with manager
Booking place in seminar
Making hotel and travel reservations
Arranging for coverage while away
Doing any preparatory work
Checking with manager for items he feels
you should be looking at in seminar

This is a relatively pleasant decision to implement. When the decision is not so pleasant, as in having to terminate an employee, for example, beware of procrastination. Without the implementation, decision making is only a paper exercise.

DEFINING THE PROBLEM

Now let's look at the problem-solving process. As you saw in the beginning of the chapter, it usually starts differently. For example, your manager calls you into his office and says: "It seems to me that the branch office reports aren't coming in as regularly as I would like. Would you look into it and see what's happening?"

This is how most problem solving starts. There is a vague awareness in someone's mind that something is not going exactly as it should. At this stage of the process, there is a great temptation to jump to a simple solution. For example: "Since the branch reports aren't coming in, I'd better send out a memo to all the branches reminding them of the monthly deadline." This approach is a mistake. At this point you don't know what the problem is—or whether there is one at all. A hasty memo might offend branches that are sending their information in on time. Others might not know what you're talking about. You have to take some time to define what the problem really is before you can solve it.

The best way to explore and define a problem is to play detective. You want to find out everything you can about the problem so that you can focus in on its real nature. The poet Rudyard Kipling gives us an excellent approach: "I have six honest serving men. They taught me all I know. Their names are who and what and when and where and why and how." In our example, some questions to which you might want to find answers are:

Who (which branches) is involved in the problem? Who at each branch is responsible for sending the reports out?

What do the branches think about these reports? Do they know how they're used? Do they have any use for them?

When are the reports coming in late? All the time or at certain times of the year? When did this lateness start? Did something else happen at the same time?

Where is the problem? Are all branches sending in late reports or just a few?
Why do some branches send in reports on time and others not? Why is it important that they send them in?
How long are the reports? How many are late? How often?

You would be looking at data and talking to people to find the answers. On the basis of your investigation, you may come up with any of these as the real problem:

How to motivate a few branches to get reports in on time as most do
How to find an alternative means of reporting branch activities
How to streamline the report form
No problem—temporary and ending

For purposes of discussion, let's say that you've uncovered a situation like this: Most branches are late in getting their reports in. There is a general feeling among them that it's just more "paper" that the head office digests. In reality the reports are extremely useful, but their form is outdated and clumsy. You decide that the best expression of your desired end result is:

How to influence branch offices to get monthly reports in on time

MORE ON THE DECISION-MAKING PROCESS

Once you have defined and clarified the problem, you follow the usual decision-making process. The next step, then, would be to generate alternative solutions. Remember, go for quantity. See how many you can come up with and then compare yours with the following list of alternative actions.

Get the branches involved in revising the report form
Use positive reinforcement when reports come in on time
Feed back data to show importance of reports
Have a contest
Clarify expectations to branches
Visit each branch and personally encourage promptness
Punish those who send late reports
Send reminders before they're due

Depending on what your manager expected from you, you could give him your results at this stage, or you could carry your work a step further to recommend a specific action.

To choose the best alternative, you might use a decision matrix. Your criteria could be cost, time to get results, acceptance by those involved, and similar criteria. You might also try a pros and cons method. List the pros and cons of each alternative. You can even add a weighted factor to each. For example:

Pros and cons of clarifying expectations

Pros		Cons	
+2	easy	−3	has been tried before
+2	little cost	−4	tends to be short-lived
+4		−7	

The numbers are your own arbitrary decision on how important each factor is, based on a scale of 1 (no importance) to 5 (great importance). This particular alternative seems to have more against it than for it.

You could also use the process of elimination to get rid of some alternatives that are least feasible. This would cut down the field for your consideration.

So far we've talked primarily about a logical approach. Don't discount your other resources. In Chapter 1, I mentioned women's edge in intuition. Since intuition or "gut feel" decisions may be the result of data that aren't yet conscious, they can be as valid as any other decisions. Intuition can be a good way, too, of cross-checking a logical approach. Using a matrix, or pros and cons, you come up with one alternative with a higher positive number than all the others. Ask yourself how you *feel* about that choice.

You may find that for many problems the best decision is a combination of alternatives. For example, in this case the combination of branch involvement in changing the form and feeding back data will probably have the best long-range possibility of effecting a change.

Once your decision is made, you will want to get the go-ahead for implementation. There is often a "best time" for putting a decision into effect. Especially if the decision involves a change effort, don't load too much on a group that has recently been through a difficult time. Do take time to plan your implementation.

What steps do you have to go through in what order? Who else will be involved in implementing the decision? What is a reasonable time frame? How will you measure your progress? And what could go wrong?

This last question is extremely important. It isn't being negative; it's a recognition that Murphy's law does exist. You've probably heard of Murphy's law: If anything can go wrong, it will. I didn't make it up; I just live with it like everybody else. When planning an implementation ask yourself what could go wrong and what you could do to stop it from happening. This is an excellent way of anticipating possible problems and making sure they don't really happen.

THE CREATIVE INPUT

Do you consider yourself creative? No, you say, you're an assistant, not an artist. Sure, you may dabble in some artistic hobby, but what does that have to do with your job? Actually, quite a bit.

Recently a lot of work has been done studying the human brain and thinking processes. What is coming out of these studies is that all of us have two different kinds of brain functions in the two halves of our brains. In most people the left brain is the seat of logical, analytical, verbal thinking; the right brain enables us to think in creative, intuitive, visual ways. In most people, either one or the other side of the brain is more developed. But all of us can develop both types of thinking further.

Logical thinking is extremely useful and is valued in the business world. Unfortunately, though, logical thinking tends to be limited. On the basis of our life experience we all have short-cut guidelines laid down in our logical brain: when I have an A problem I do a B solution. That's a quick way to solve problems, but not completely effective. Sometimes what seems to be an A problem is really a G problem; that means a B solution doesn't quite fit. Or maybe the B solution is okay, but a newer type of solution, even a Q, could be better. What I'm illustrating here is the tendency of logic to limit our decision-making ability in two areas of the process: defining problems and generating alternatives.

In both these areas you want your brain to "reach" for newness and/or quantity. The chief impediment to creativity is that most of us have learned that logic is good and grown-up whereas creativity is bad, childlike, and unsuited to the business world. Be aware, when you are problem solving, of the little "messages" that may arise in your mind: "I should do this. Creativity is silly; stick to the facts. In the past I've always solved this problem this way."

I want to prove to all of you that you have already done some creative thinking. Let's say you have a problem. It could be a problem at work or something to do with a hobby at home. You try everything you can to solve it. Nothing. So you figuratively—or literally—throw it down in disgust and walk away. Forget it.

Then, without your thinking about it, an hour later, a day later, a week later, a solution comes to you. (In the comic strips, the light bulb goes on in the person's head.) That's creativity. By going away from the problem you freed your mind to "play with" solutions until it came up with a novel one.

In the problem-solving process, creativity is most useful in the definition of problems and the generation of alternatives. When faced with a problem, beware of jumping to look at solutions. Take time to define the problem. Look at it from as many different vantage points as you can.

MANY WAYS OF LOOKING AT A PROBLEM

There is a classic exercise in creative problem definition that you might like to try. In this case, the owners of a large office building were receiving a great many complaints from their tenants about the shortage of elevators. The companies that rented space in the building told the owners that there was too much waiting time for their employees and clients. They wanted more elevators. The problem as originally defined was "how to increase the number of elevators in the building." This definition would require a very expensive solution.

But maybe the problem could be redefined. Take a few minutes and write down as many ways as you can think of to express the problem. Let yourself go. Stretch your mind. Then come back to the book.

Here are some of the ways this problem could be redefined:

How to change people flow
How to find alternatives to elevators
How to make elevators more efficient
How to reallocate office space
How to reduce complaints

Now let's see how a change in *definition* of the problem can lead to more and varied solutions.

Problem	*Possible solutions*
Change people flow	Flexitime
Find alternatives to elevators	Escalators for lower floors
	Promotion of use of stairs—fitness?
Make elevators more efficient	Expresses and locals
	Operators on elevators
Reallocate office space	Tenants with most people flow resettled on lower floors
Reduce complaints	Creation of some kind of diversion at elevators—bulletin boards, for example

Do you see how it works? Supposedly this problem really occurred. And the way it was solved was related to the problem of how to reduce complaints. The management of the building did what many hotels do. It had mirrors installed by the elevator banks. And complaints dropped.

Turning Out the Alternatives

The term I like to use here is "generate." At this stage of the problem-solving or decision-making process, you want to generate—in the sense of a machine turning out product—quantities of ideas. The more possible solutions you have, the more probable it is that you will come up with the best one. There are two creative techniques you can use, either by yourself or in a group, to help your mind come up with ideas.

Creative Technique No. 1. Brainstorming

This is the "granddaddy" of creative techniques and still a very useful one. A group involved in a problem-solving session is ready to list possible solutions to the problem. The group sets a time limit, 15 to 30 minutes, and appoints one person to write the ideas down on a flip chart. It agrees that during the time period any idea that comes up will be written down. *And no criticism of ideas is allowed.*

If you've ever been in a group, presented an idea, and had someone comment that your idea was unworkable or unsuitable or even stupid, you know how criticism stops ideas. You probably sat silent the rest of the meeting.

In a brainstorming session, once the time period is up and all ideas have been written down, the group evaluates the ideas. It may pick out one or a combination that will best solve its problem. Please note that brainstorming is not just "crazy ideas." The ideas are evaluated—but only after they are generated in a free atmosphere.

Brainstorming can also be done by an individual. Next time you have a problem, take about ten minutes and write down as many ways you can think of to solve it. Beware of a tendency to criticize even when brainstorming on your own: "I shouldn't write that down." "That won't work." "That's silly." Apply the "no criticism" rule to yourself. You will come up with many more ideas.

Creative Technique No. 2. Random Word

Just as brainstorming is practically a classic approach to creative problem solving, random word is one of the newest. It can be used in conjunction with brainstorming or instead of it. It's a technique designed to help your mind ramble—get away from "tried and true" solutions.

The group—or you alone—is ready to discuss alternatives. You pick up a book you have, open to a page, and read the first word you see. Let's say, for example, that you are meeting with a group of assistants to find a solution to the common problem of decreased motivation in your junior people. The first word you see on the page is "butterfly." What does "butterfly" say to you about motivation? Take a few minutes and write down your ideas. Here's a sample of my associations:

Color—office environment—brighten it up
Flight—freedom—more independence
Net—closed in—tight rules—resentment
Net—close group—promote teams to do work
Varied—many kinds—different people—different needs—find out
Caterpillar—cocoon—waiting to turn into butterflies—potential

When you run out of ideas, choose another word. Random word is an excellent technique for getting to new, different, and varied solutions to your problems.

Increasing General Creativity

In addition to specific techniques for creative problem solving, I recommend some general ways of improving your creativity. As children we are extremely creative; as we gain logical thinking through the education process we tend to lost the creativity. We can recover it. Some general ways to do that are:

Have a "honeybee" mind. Read everything that comes across your desk. Go to the library once in a while and sift through some magazines that have nothing to do with your industry. You will pick up ideas that will become useful.

Do puzzles. There are books of mind-bender types of puzzles that will "exercise" your creative muscles.

Practice. Develop a "bug list," things that drive you crazy on the job. Periodically try to generate ways to deal with one of these bugs. You will find a great deal of useful knowledge within yourself.

SYNTHESIS

Putting it all together, I see problem solving and decision making as most effective when carried out with a combination of logical and creative, or left-brain and right-brain, processes. Figure 7 puts these in visual form.

Release your mind to explore and define the problem in many ways. Switch to the left brain to set up logical criteria by which to evaluate the solution. Turn on the creative generator to get ideas on how to solve the problem. Use a logical decision matrix or pros and cons to choose the best solution. You may use intuition as an adjunct if this resource proves effective for you. Methodically plan how you are going to carry out your decision.

The ability to solve problems and make sound decisions is a vital skill to anyone in management. But even the most skilled cannot be guaranteed of making the right decision all the time. The key to effectiveness is learning from your experience. Get into the habit of evaluating the results of your decision making. When you make a

Figure 7: The problem-solving process.

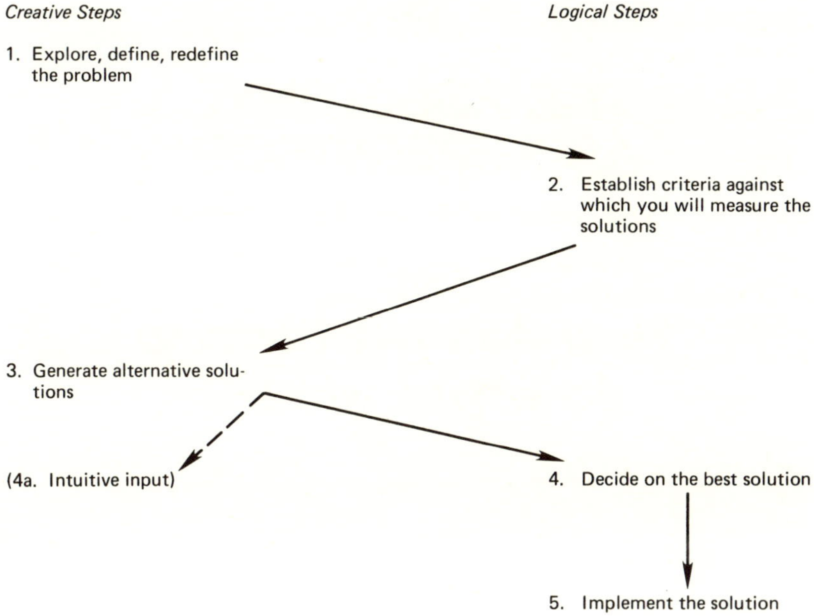

good one, ask yourself why and how you can repeat the success. If you make a bad decision, don't sweep it under the rug. Learn from it. What should you do next time—or avoid doing—to reach a better decision?

9

THE ASSISTANT AS SUPERVISOR

or "How do I get them to do what I want?"

Increasingly, the assistant of today has, as a large part of her job, the supervision of other junior people in the office. If she is a capable leader, she will find that her subordinates extend her own ability. If she is a poor leader, she will find her staff to be a constant source of irritation. Rather then making her job easier, they will make it harder. In this chapter I'd like to share with you some of my ideas on what supervision is and how it can best be carried out.

LEADERSHIP

Hundreds of books have been written on the nature of leadership and it still hasn't been defined clearly. Instead of trying to pinpoint exactly what leadership is in the role of the supervisor, I'd like to give you four ideas that, taken together, make up leadership for me. The four ideas are summed up in the word LEAD.

Leadership is determined by followership. There was a time in organizations, and in society, when the label "boss" or "leader" was enough to give the holder of the label influence over others. But that has changed; our society has changed. Today the followers choose a leader, even in organizations. That means that your subordinates actively, although often unconsciously, make judgments on whether you fit their perception of a leader. If you do not, you will get limited acceptance and limited productivity from them.

Education is the foundation of leadership. The supervisor of today influences her subordinates by moving them in certain directions. She doesn't push; she doesn't pull; she doesn't prod. To be effective, she must show the employee what is expected of her and then help the employee to achieve it through training, reinforcement, and appraisal. The leader is a guide more than anything else.

Adaptation to the individual is necessary. Every one of us, when presented with a so-called leader, wants to know "What's in this for me? How will this relationship work out for me?" The answer to that is always an individual one. In Chapter 3 we looked at the hierarchy of needs, an excellent motivation model that shows the common needs people have. It also implies that each person has an individual profile in terms of needs. A large part of your ability as a supervisor is made up of your willingness and capability to clue into the needs of each of your subordinates.

Dynamism is part of the process. One of the greatest challenges of supervision is that you can never sit down and say you've done your job. You never know a subordinate fully or, if you think you do, she decides to change. You change too, and that affects your behavior. Supervision means working out your needs, your staff's needs, your boss's needs, and your organization's needs and weaving them all together to achieve the objective.

YOUR IDEAL EMPLOYEE

If you supervise others, you probably have somewhere in your mind a picture of the ideal employee. If you only had employees like that, what a supervisor you would be! But, of course, ideal employees are not waiting somewhere for you to come and pick them up. The effective employee is the result of a number of effective behaviors on the part of the supervisor. Some of the most important are:

Selection
Orientation
Training
Delegation
Appraisal

Let's explore each of these areas to give you some help in producing as many of these "ideal" employees as you can.

Selection

This is your first step toward getting the effective employee. If the raw material isn't the best you can get, the chances of achieving effectiveness in that employee are small. The selection process breaks down into analyzing the job, recruiting, and interviewing.

Before you ever set out to find someone to fit a job, you must know what the job is. What kinds of skills are needed? What education level is best? What kind of work atmosphere are you offering? What kinds of attitudes are necessary? It's relatively easy to decide on the skills you're looking for, but be aware, too, of some of the peripheral parts of the job that can affect your success in selection. For example, is this a job that requires hours of detail work? You need someone who can handle that concentration, away from people, comfortably. Is this a job that has periods of intense activity? You need someone who can handle pressure. If you've had a high turnover in the job, ask yourself why. How did those people not fit the job?

When recruiting you sometimes have a free hand, sometimes not. If you do, look at your own experience to find the best method of recruiting. Where have you, or your organization, tended to get the best employees? Rather than recommending agencies or newspaper ads or personal referrals, I'd say your own experience is most telling. And don't discount the "walk-in"; this person has already shown a certain spunk by coming in cold. She can make a very good employee.

The employee interview is mainly an information-gathering session. You want to find out how well this person fits the job. Like any interview, it should start out on a comfortable note. Pick out some interesting item on her application form and talk about it a little—her high school, a hobby, or a special award.

In the interview, you will want to find out about this prospective employee's education, work experience, and attitudes. During the interview beware of these common mistakes:

- Don't talk too much. When you're talking, you're not getting information.

- Don't ask leading questions. How would you answer: "Have you had a lot of math in school?" You know what the questioner wants. That doesn't give real information.
- Don't ask too many direct questions. "What is your typing speed?" will give you a simple answer. "Tell me about your typing" will encourage the person to talk about her speed, likes and dislikes, and experience. You will get data on attitudes as well as straight facts.

If the personnel department or your boss hires people for you, do your best to get input into the process, especially if you've had problems with turnover. You could use that as a selling point to show how your intimate knowledge of the job requirements would be helpful in selection.

Orientation

First impressions count—in meeting people and in orienting new employees. This is an opportunity that is usually wasted by the supervisor. During orientation you probably spend most of the time giving the new employee facts on lunches and hours and things like that. Use this time, too, to clarify your expectations of the employee and what she, in turn, can expect from you:

> We're happy to have you working here. We feel that you have the ability to do the job and we will train you so that you have all you need to be successful. You'll find that we often work hard in this department—especially around the end of the month—but we also reward well. You'll find it a pleasant atmosphere, friendly, and one in which your ideas will be listened to.
>
> We expect our employees to be out no more than eight days a year. It's important to come to work on a regular basis; we depend on you and what you produce. We expect you to produce at a rate that we've established; it's well within your ability. But we don't expect that right away. I want you to see me as the person who is responsible for helping you to get your work done. Feel free to ask me anything you want. Now let's talk about what you'll be doing for the first week. . . .

Help the new person hit it off right with her fellow workers. Introduce her as someone who will be helpful to them and brings needed skills to the department.

Training

Assumptions are often made when training an employee. These assumptions, if acted on, can make the training process relatively ineffective.

- Don't assume the new employee knows how to do something—or the way it must be done in your department—just because she has used that skill in another job.
- Don't assume she knows nothing. Every employee walks into the organization with varied experience behind her.
- Don't assume that every person is the same—and can be trained in exactly the same way.
- Don't assume that your best worker is necessarily the person to whom you should delegate training. There is often a difference between job ability and training ability.
- Don't assume that telling an employee what you want done and then walking away is training.

Proper training is extremely important. Often, a supervisor will think that an employee who is not performing well in a job has a motivation or attitude problem. Sometimes it is neither of these, but an ability problem. If a person doesn't know how to do a job, she cannot be motivated to do it, nor will she feel comfortable with it. Here is my ten-step plan for effective training:

1. Decide what you want to teach and set standards. What do you expect the employee to be able to do after she is trained? At what rate? Speed? Quantity? Quality? If you don't know what you expect the trained employee to be able to do, you cannot communicate it to her.

2. Plan to treat the learner as an individual. What kind of trainee do you have? If she is a shy, inexperienced person, you must plan a very supportive, yet direct, approach: "This is what you do—and I know you can do it." If you have an individual with a lot of experience who sees herself as competent, you will take a more collegial approach: "Why don't you tell me the kinds of things you've done with this machine; then we'll look at what we use it for here." In general, the more ability and independence the employee shows, the more listening and guiding, as opposed to telling and directing, you will want to do.

3. Tell the trainee what you expect and when. Most new people

on the job assume that they have to know how to do everything tomorrow. That creates fear and tension, which can be barriers to training. Tell the employee what you want and when: "With your ability, I feel you will be able to handle this perfectly in a few weeks."

4. Give a general outline of the material first. Did you ever try to do a jigsaw puzzle without first looking at the picture on the box? Almost impossible. In the same way, before training others, give them an overall view of what they will be learning:

> First I'm going to show you how to divide the invoices into three piles. Then I'll show you where to get the information to check them against. And finally we'll look at how you put the information on these sheets.

5. Show and tell. If you want someone to remember what you tell her, show what you tell at the same time. You can double her retention by using some kind of visual stimuli added to your words. Be dramatic, even, to make your point:

> If I don't push this button first, when I push the bar, everything disappears from the screen. See? I've erased it. You don't want that to happen to the data you're working on, so remember to push the button first.

6. Give the "whys." The training process is full of techniques designed to ensure that the learner will learn and will retain the new knowledge. If she understands why she is doing something, your new employee will be more likely to remember how to do it:

> You may think it's overly picky to put these items in order at this point. But you will find that when you get to column 4, if you haven't got them in order, you'll have to stop and do it. You'll lose your train of thought and make more mistakes.

7. Watch while the employee performs the job. It may seem simple to you, but you don't really know if the employee "got" what you thought you communicated until you check it out. Tell what's right; tell what's wrong. Even if there's very little of the former and a lot of the latter, start on a positive note: "Your first step was correct but then you skipped the second step and got lost. Let's start again."

8. Ask questions. As in any case in which you are asking for feedback, don't give the impression you're checking to see if the individual was listening. Instead, put any lack of communication ability on yourself: "I want to make sure I've fully explained the system. Where

would you file this paper?" A thinking person is a learning person who will retain the learning.

9. Put the learner on her own gradually. How gradually depends on her ability and the difficulty of the task. You want to know how she's doing, but you don't want to hover over her. The more capable and/or self-confident the learner is, the more freedom you want to give her.

10. Remember—and tell the learner about—the "learning curve." People tend not to learn at an even rate. If they did, and if we were to plot their learning against time, the graph would look like this:

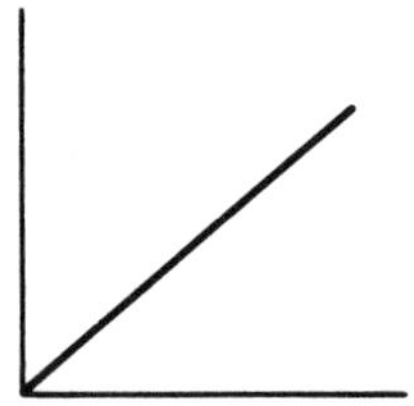

Instead, people tend to learn in stops and starts, plateaus and jumps, like this:

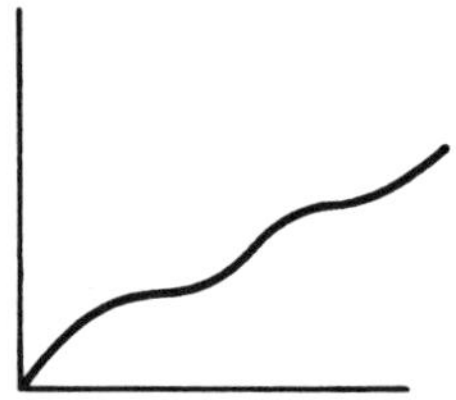

If you and your learner expect that at some point she will probably say "I thought I knew this. Now I don't know anything," you'll be prepared to deal with it. You can help the employee by telling her it's normal and if she keeps at it she'll be better than ever.

The use of these ten training steps will help ensure that your employees know how to do the job for which they have been hired.

Delegation

From the time you first enter management ranks, you hear the word "delegation." Although the word is familiar, delegation itself is one of the most difficult skills most supervisors have to learn. As a supervisor, you have been put in charge of other people because you were seen as competent in your work, but in supervising others, you must be willing and able to go beyond doing the work and move, instead, to delegating this work to others.

As many of you have already discovered, there is an enormous difference between doing something yourself and getting other people to do it. I'm going to give you some tips to make the delegation process easier for you.

1. *Decide what you want*. Notice that the first step in the delegation process is the same as the first step in the training process, the selection process, and the communication process. You can't possibly get the results you want in any of these processes unless you know in your own mind what you expect. Figuring it out doesn't have to be a long process. Just take a minute to think about what results you want and what limitations, if any, there are.

2. *Select the right person*. Who is the right person? At this point many of you can actually picture a real person, some employee of yours who has the ability and maybe even the right attitude to do the job. Very often this *is* the right person to whom to delegate. But be careful. You have other employees, too. "But," you say, "the others are not as competent." That's where your ability as a supervisor comes in. It is your job progressively, slowly, in a step-by-step, partial way to delegate to these others so that eventually they can be as effective as your star employee. Maybe that sounds idealistic, but the job of the supervisor *is* to develop others.

3. *Take note of personal preferences*. One of the cornerstones of all organizations is job definition—certain positions to handle certain work. When you can, however, try to delegate to the individual. One person loves to file. Let her. Another finds statistical typing interesting. Let her do it. If people want to switch elements of their jobs, that can be very motivating for them, a way of breaking away from the routine.

4. *Communicate the required results*. If you are clear in your own mind as to what you want, you can communicate it effectively. If there is only one way to do the job, say so. If you're looking for new methods, make that clear. In general, aim for flexibility in this area. You may be pleasantly surprised at the good ideas you see coming out of your people.

This is also a good time to use the communication technique of feedback. "What is your understanding of what I'm expecting?" People will not often ask questions if they don't understand something. By asking them to feed back their understanding of your communication, you can pick up any misunderstandings.

5. *Clarify your expectations*. One of the most motivating elements of supervision, and one that has been proved out in study after study, is the concept of high expectations. If you have clarified what you want and given the person the information and tools she needs to do it, you can expect good results. If you approach an individual with an "I don't know if you can handle this" attitude, you will communicate your apprehension. Then neither of you will be surprised when she fails. Use the "I know you can do it and I will help you" approach. You will get better results.

6. *Show the importance of the task*. Why does it have to be done? What is going to be done with it? Who is going to use it? How does it fit in with the work of the department? One of the difficulties in organizations today is that people tend to get lost in the crowd. If a person feels that she's just one more gear in the big machine, she won't think it's important to do a good job. What does it matter? You want to get people away from that attitude.

7. *Control the work*. That doesn't mean holding on with tight reins. It does mean knowing what is going on and taking corrective action if necessary. For some employees control is checking periodically. For others, it's "I'll see you when you're finished. If you have questions, ask me." It depends on the difficulty of the task, the ability of the person doing the work, and her own preference. Some people want the supervisor near. They feel more secure. Others want independence. Know your people and act accordingly.

8. *Appraise and give feedback*. Do the results match what you thought you'd get? If not, why not? Were you not clear on what you wanted? Did you choose the wrong person? Did you not explain all the limitations? Did you have low expectations? Did you control too much or too little?

If you get something different from what you expected, is it wrong—or just different? It doesn't have to be wrong just because it's not the way you would have done it. If you got good results, don't keep silent because your employee was supposed to do a good job. Remember the uses of positive stroking. There's nothing wrong with saying to a good employee periodically: "Thanks again. You always do a good job." If your employees see that good work gets lots of attention, they will tend to be motivated to produce good work.

Appraisal

One of the most difficult parts of the job for the administrative assistant who supervises others is appraisal. The assistant may see the appraisal interview as a time when she has to judge others, when there may be arguments, when she's in an uncomfortable situation.

Knowing how to appraise can make the situation easier. Let's talk about the important things for you to remember in an appraisal interview. These are preparation, tone, communication techniques, and focus.

Preparation

I've seen offices in which appraisal interviews are carried out something like this: The assistant or supervisor says to a subordinate: "Helen, I've got a few extra minutes. Let's get your appraisal out of the way." No wonder appraisal is a waste of time for both of them!

To give a good appraisal requires preparation on both your part and the employee's part. Most of your preparation is doing some hard thinking about this employee and the work she has been doing. Look over your record of her work for the past six months or year—whatever the time period for appraisals is. The record I'm talking about doesn't have to be extensive. But as a supervisor you should make it a habit to keep notes on critical incidents, both positive and negative, for your employees. That way you have data for the actual appraisal.

Some of you work in companies in which appraisal involves a form of some kind. Some common types of appraisal forms are:

1. Rating the employee on items such as work quantity, work quality, punctuality, initiative, and similar data. Ratings may be expressed as 1 to 5; A to D; or Excellent, Good, Fair, Poor.
2. Evaluating the employee's work according to her job description.
3. Comparing the employee's performance to some standard objective.

If you don't have a form, that doesn't mean you can't appraise. As long as you have some basis on which to evaluate job performance—and have communicated what that basis is to the employee—you can appraise her performance validly. A great deal of the unpleasantness in appraisal interviews occurs because the supervisor assumes the employee knows what is expected of her and the employee really doesn't. That leads to a lot of communications of this type: "You should have. . . ." "But I didn't know. . . ." "But you should have known. . . ." "But I thought. . . ."

The simplest way to prepare if you do not have a form to follow is to ask yourself two questions about the employee's work: (1) In what areas has this employee been doing at least satisfactory work? Excellent work? (2) In what areas can this employee improve? How?

The second part is alerting the employee to the interview and trying to get her involved in and committed to it. "Helen, since I'm doing appraisal interviews next week, I'd like to set aside some time to talk over your job with you. Tuesday mornings are not a particularly busy time, are they?" You could go beyond this and ask her to write down her own perceptions on the kind of job she's been doing. If you have a particular appraisal form, ask her to fill it out for herself. There is a definite trend in organizations today to have employees give input into their own appraisals. It gets the supervisor away from the "Now I'm going to judge you" feeling and approach.

Tone

Most employees enter the appraisal situation expecting to be criticized and even demeaned. You want to start off the interview on a note that will show the employee this is not the case. I think you have to deal with the employee's feeling at this point and set the ground rules for the interview:

1. Talk for a minute or two about something of interest to the employee—family, hobby, vacation. Don't drag this out too long.
2. Go on to reflect her feelings: "You haven't had an appraisal interview with me before and must be wondering what it's going to be like."
3. Tell the procedure: "We're going to spend about half an hour talking about your job, both the areas in which you're doing well and those in which you may need to improve. I'll be giving you my observations on your work and I'll be listening quite a lot to what you think."

At this point your employee should be reasonably comfortable and ready to proceed with the interview.

Communication Techniques

The third element of a good appraisal interview is the type of communication used in it. Think of the communication techniques in terms of twos: two types of communication—telling and listening. The appraisal interview is an excellent time for you to be assertive. A combination of I-talk and listening will be very effective. Here are some examples:

"I feel your typing could be neater. How do you see your typing?"

"I think your strongest job skill is your organizing ability. What do you see as your greatest strength?"

"What are some areas in which you feel you need improvement? I agree that your work with numbers isn't as good as it could be, but I feel there's more of a problem with your cooperation in the group."

Two types of feedback, positive and negative. You don't want your employees to associate the appraisal interview with criticism alone. You also don't want to sidestep problem areas that exist. Some employees you appraise will have many pluses and few negatives; others will be just the opposite. Your feedback during the interview ought to be some combination of these two aspects of the person's job.

"I'm very pleased with the way you've learned to use the new typewriter so quickly."

"I'm concerned about your lateness record."

"You have a wonderful ability to work well with others."

"Let's talk about your accuracy rate. It's not up to standard."

"Thank you for putting so much effort into that rush job last week."

Two kinds of listening, to the content and to the feelings. We've explained the many kinds of listening in Chapter 6. In an appraisal interview your purpose is to guide the employee into looking at her own work and making committed decisions on how she can improve it. That means you want to have her talk about the job; use active listening techniques to accomplish this.

"In general, then, you feel that your greatest difficulty is the pace of the work."

"You're saying that you like the job but it gets boring at times."

"You're unhappy sometimes?"

"This job isn't what you expected."

Don't forget to listen to the feelings, too. You want your employee to feel comfortable, to feel understood, to feel free to talk.

"I see how frustrating it is."
"I realize how difficult it is working under these conditions."
"You feel torn between two aspects of the job?"
"You seem somehow dissatisfied with what I'm suggesting."

Focus

Probably the biggest problem with appraisal interviews is that they turn into blame sessions: "You should have. . . ." "Why didn't you?" "That was unacceptable." The purpose of appraisal is to create a better future for you and your employee. The past can be used as evidence, but the interview must eventually be brought around to what is going to be done in the future to improve this employee's handling of the job.

Specific goals and follow-up are the two elements to be considered here. Don't send an employee off with only her promise that she'll "do better." You will have accomplished nothing. Instead, decide on a few important objectives and a time period for them:

"You're going to use your dictionary to check spelling. And I'm going to keep a weekly record of your accuracy and feed the results back to you. We agree that you can cut these errors to 3 percent in a month."

"So you've agreed that your absence record is far above average, and we've set a goal of no more than two absences within the next three months. We'll meet briefly each week to look at how you're doing."

Remember that a large part of your effectiveness in the appraisal interview stems from what you do long before the interview. You must know what you expect from each employee; you have to communicate these expectations to each. You should keep some kind of observation notes on each employee; you can then compare her behavior with your standards. Make the person feel good in the interview, but don't sidestep problem areas.

Organizations are full of deadwood—people who don't do their jobs—because their supervisors didn't want to criticize them. Keep the criticism objective. ("This is the standard. This is how you've been doing.") Help the employee to go beyond it. ("I know you can do better and I'll help you do it.") The appraisal interview is one of those aspects of the supervisor's job that is necessary but difficult. Knowing how to do it and following the guidelines can make it easier.

ASSISTANT MODELS TO AVOID

As a way of bringing together all these ideas on better supervision for the administrative assistant, I'd like to introduce you to four assistants. I want you to meet them and know them because I don't want you to be like them. Each is an ineffective leader of others in some way. May I introduce:

Heavy-Handed Hanna

The only communication technique Hanna knows is telling people what to do. She is completely inflexible and open to only one person's ideas—her own. Somewhere along the way Hanna got the idea that being a supervisor of others was something like being a top sergeant in the army: selection is drafting; orientation is boot camp (the weak go under); delegation is barking orders; and appraisal is a court-martial. Hanna's leadership style doesn't work in today's organization.

Keep-It-to-Herself Kitty

Kitty believes in the old saying: "If you want a good job done, do it yourself." She finds great satisfaction in doing things herself; the trouble is her employees are underused and unmotivated because of it. Kitty feels that people today don't know how to work any more. Of course, she never gives them the chance. Kitty is usually harried because she is doing her employees' jobs; she has little time for what she's supposed to be doing. Kitty doesn't know that employee development is one of the supervisor's most important jobs.

Mother Martha

Martha is a nice woman, but being a mother to her employees is *so* taxing. She takes care of them; she tells them how to do everything (nicely, but clearly her way); she gets completely involved in their private lives; she cleans up their messes when they do a bad job. After all, a mother doesn't desert her children, does she? Martha sighs a lot and wishes she didn't have so much responsibility. But how can you give responsibility to these "kids"? Unfortunately, Martha has taken a good thing—nurturing—and turned it into a crutch.

Just-the-Facts Jessica

Jessica thinks that all this "people stuff" is so much nonsense. All you have to do to be a good supervisor is make sure the job is defined clearly, and the employee will do it. Jessica runs by papers, procedures, rules, and regulations. Her employees are just so many results-producing machines: program them with a job description and see them go! If Jessica were "supervising" robots, she might be successful. But people can't be—and won't be—turned into machines.

Supervising others is one of the most challenging—and most rewarding—aspects of the assistant's job. If you enjoy it and are good at it, you may be thinking about career growth into higher management ranks. In the next chapter we'll explore those possibilities.

10

GETTING AHEAD

or "Some people have all the luck."

In a recent "Peanuts" cartoon, Charlie Brown is seen sitting with a mopey look on his face. Linus comes along and asks what he's doing. "I just thought I'd stand here and watch the world go by," says Charlie. In the next frame we see Charlie with a bewildered look saying, "It never came by."

That cartoon says a lot about the way most people look at so-called career planning. Wait . . . hope . . . dream . . . maybe you'll be lucky. Women, particularly, tend to see it that way. Just look at the learning experiences of women as we discussed them in Chapter 1. You will realize that the traditional woman never saw herself in charge of her own life. She was passed from father to brother to husband for decisions without responsibility. We live in a much different world today, but many women still look at their success, or lack of it, as mainly a matter of luck. Fortunately that is not so; one's career success can be influenced greatly by purposeful action.

WHAT DO YOU KNOW ABOUT CAREER PLANNING?

Check your understanding of what career planning is. In the following exercise decide whether you think each statement is true or false.

	True	False
1. Hard work will guarantee success.	____	____
2. A good boss can make or break a career.	____	____
3. Goal setting is an important part of career planning.	____	____
4. To be successful, you have to live, eat, and breathe your work and exclude everything else.	____	____
5. The higher you set your sights, the higher you will get, so everyone should set out to be president of the company.	____	____
6. Risk taking is a necessary part of a successful career.	____	____
7. Luck has no place in career planning.	____	____
8. Career planning starts with deciding what you want to do.	____	____

Here are the answers:

1. *False*. Organizations are full of people who thought this. I don't mean that hard work isn't necessary. It is. I mean that hard work is not enough. Just as aimless busyness is not the ideal in time management, hard work without a consideration of the political factors in organizations is a poor form of career management.
2. *True*. A number of studies of successful executives have shown this: The major factor to which they attribute their success is that at one time they each worked for a boss who taught, led, and supported them into doing things they had thought they couldn't do. Many assistants can remember the opposite kind of boss—the one who wanted to keep them where they were because of their usefulness. That type of boss is a barrier.
3. *True*. Direction, risk, and step-by-step development are all implied in goal setting. Of course, the goals have to be set in a certain way to make them work. Relatively undemanding goals will not "stretch" the individual and make her grow. Unrealistically high goals will only cause frustration.
4. *Sometimes true, sometimes false*, depending on the individual. Most successful women have had to put long hours and lots of energy into their success. Some of them have found that being without a husband, children, hobbies, or many friends helped them to do this. Others—including myself—have found that a

family life, friends, and nonwork-related activities have broadened them, cut down on stress, and perhaps even improved them in their jobs. You have to know what you want in life.

5. *True and false*. It is true that the higher you set your sights, the greater the probability of your reaching those high levels. If you set out to be a supervisor, you will probably go no further. If you set out to be a vice-president, you might end up being a supervisor, but you're more likely to become a manager or even a vice-president.

   It's been my experience that many women are scared away from career planning because they think it means they have to shoot for the top or they're not doing it right. I don't agree with that. I think people should aim for the very top only if they want to. What is to be avoided is setting goals so low that one ends up in a lifetime of frustration: "I can't get out of the secretarial trap." "They'll never make a woman a manager."

6. *True*. There is no such thing as a steady straight line to one's career ideal. You make stops and starts. If you decide to make a career move, it may end up being a good one or a mistake. But the chances of reaching any kind of achievement are almost nil without the willingness to try.

7. *False*. After reading my first paragraph in this chapter, you probably thought the answer to this would be true. But if you look at the life stories of famous people, you will find that elements of luck seem to be part of many of these successes. It depends on what you see as luck. Many of you have seen some of the movie musicals of the 1930s and 1940s on TV. Usually, in the story, the big star of a musical comedy falls sick. Her understudy, or a chorus girl, but nonetheless an unknown, fills in and becomes a star. Luck? Not really, unless you consider luck, as I do, to be a combination of preparation and opportunity.

   Opportunities come to many people: a new job, meeting an important person, heading a successful project, filling in for the star. But in each of these cases the lucky person had to make some kind of input: to be able to handle the new job well, to present some new ideas to the important person, to carry through the successful project with her own skills, to be a great performer.

8. *False*. Many people have absolutely no idea what they want to do, so how can they decide where they want to go? There's a step

that comes before that—which brings us to my approach to career planning. It is built on three steps. Prepare yourself now to do some soul-searching, take some risks, and take a lot of responsibility for your own life.

THE STEPS OF CAREER PLANNING

The three major steps of career planning are the same steps necessary to any kind of planning. You have to answer the following questions:

Where are you now?
Where do you want to go?
How do you get there?

Many people would start with question 2, but if you do that the choice of destinations becomes limitless and therefore difficult. You can't know where and how you want to go unless you look first at your starting point. Let's use an analogy to explain the process: planning a vacation.

Before you decide on a destination you probably go though a series of self-questions. You ask yourself the kind of vacation you like—sightseeing, relaxing on the beach, sports. You ask yourself what you have done before that you would like to do again. You ask yourself what you have always wanted to try.

You probably also look at what is available. You might read through brochures you've obtained from a travel bureau. Maybe there are some travel bargains that interest you. You have to consider your resources—how much time you have at what time of the year; how much money you have to spend.

You may talk to friends and see what they've done on vacation and enjoyed. One might send you in the direction of a special deal—lend you a cottage, for example, or just recommend a good travel agent. Only after you do all this research are you ready to decide where you want to go on vacation. Once you decide on the location, you have to make arrangements: carriers, hotel, itinerary, activities.

Effective career planning goes through the same steps but can be done in two time focuses: interim job planning and lifetime career planning. Interim job planning is a short-term type of planning designed to help you improve yourself in your present job. I recommend it if you either are positive you are already in your ideal job or are not quite ready to embark on lifetime career planning. (I consider the latter a temporary state. Don't fool yourself into waiting until retirement to plan your career.)

Asking yourself where you are now means assessing yourself in your current job. The second part of interim planning is setting short-term goals in relation to what you learned in your assessment. These may be self-improvement goals in areas in which you need improvement or they may be goals for the next job step you can take. How you get there is answered by deciding on a plan to reach these goals.

In order to focus on lifetime career planning, you must first decide what you like doing. What have your job experiences been and how did you feel about them? What have you always wanted to do? What proven skills do you have? You may also want to know what's available. What is the job outlook for careers that interest you? What is it really like to work in these jobs?

On the basis of all that research you will reach the point at which you can begin to focus in on a career goal. After that come the "hows." Let's look at these three types of planning in Table 1.

Table 1.

Planning a Vacation	*Planning a Lifetime Career*	*Interim Job Planning*
Dreams Past experience Likes and dislikes	Visions Past experience Feelings Skills	Present job skills Likes and dislikes
Resources What's available Choice of location	Job outlooks Contacts in field Goals	Possible moves in organization Self-improvement or job goal
Timetable Hotels Carriers Activities	What to do When How	Courses Projects

Interim Job Planning

Now I'm going to take you through the first career process: interim job planning. Where are you now? Assess your capabilities in each of the following areas by giving yourself a rating of excellent, satisfactory, or poor:

	Excellent	*Satisfactory*	*Poor*
Organization and Time Management Skills			
For self	_____	_____	_____
For manager	_____	_____	_____
Writing Skills			
Letters	_____	_____	_____
Reports	_____	_____	_____
Human Relations Skills			
With manager	_____	_____	_____
With subordinates	_____	_____	_____
With others	_____	_____	_____
Problem-Solving Skills			
Logical	_____	_____	_____
Creative	_____	_____	_____
Verbal Communication Skills			
One-on-one	_____	_____	_____
In a group	_____	_____	_____
Public speaking	_____	_____	_____
Supervisory Skills			
Selection	_____	_____	_____
Training	_____	_____	_____
Delegation	_____	_____	_____
Appraisal	_____	_____	_____

On the basis of this self-analysis, you are ready to decide what you can be working on during the next year. Some possible goals are:

To improve general human relations through the use of stroking
To be able to write 50 percent of manager's correspondence effectively

To reorganize the office filing system
To move up from secretary to administrative assistant level with increased responsibility

Now that you have your goals, how are you going to achieve them? Not by writing the goals alone. Here you must make a plan for yourself on how you're going to reach your objectives. Some of the methods you must look at are:

Formal courses or seminars
On-the-job projects
Handling of self-barriers
Getting needed contacts

Let's look at an example of the planning procedure using our "six honest serving men."

What: To be able, within one year, to handle 50 percent of the manager's correspondence personally

Why: To improve self in a vital skill
To motiviate self through learning and increased responsibility
To make better use of manager's time

Where: Outgoing letters and memos

When: Starting now and gradually increasing over one year

Who: Myself, primarily
Enlist aid of manager

How:
1. Take a correspondence course in writing for business.
2. Start using the four guidelines on letters I now write.
3. Choose at least two other types of correspondence I feel I can write and make presentation to manager to sell the idea.
4. Once a month, review correspondence received to be familiar with good and bad writing.
5. Check within three months to see how much additional correspondence I am handling.

Interim job planning can be an excellent way for you to recapture the "excitement" of your job. The skills you improve in yourself will add to the base you already have. Such skills will be important when you are ready to look at lifetime career planning.

Lifetime Career Planning

Where Are You Now?

Career planning on this level is a very complex and time-consuming activity, but it gives the greatest payoff. I'm going to guide you through some selected exercises that will give you a good start in planning what you want to do with the rest of your work life.

John Crystal, who, with Richard Bolles, has written one of the finest books available on career planning, wrote in that book: "Most people have cut down their original dream to 1/8 of its original size and strength; hence, they are only hunting for 1/8 of their original dream with 1/8 of their heart (or guts)."

The vision, or dream, of what you would like to be is part of this first section on lifetime career planning. Also involved is an analysis of your special skills and your expectations. In general, in this section you are looking at yourself, perhaps for the first time in your life, as a resource. You must see what your hopes, your feelings, and your capabilities are.

Exercise 1. Visions. Describe your ideal job. If you could have any job in the world, what would it be like? It doesn't have to have a name, but I want you to describe it in all its details. What would you do every day? What would the environment be like? Would you work with others or alone? By what standards would your work be measured? What rewards would you receive? What challenges would you have? In this exercise, shoot for the stars. There are no barriers; you are free to create the perfect job for yourself.

Exercise 2. Past Experiences. Write down the five greatest success experiences of your life. These can be, but do not have to be, work related. Describe in detail what you *had to do* to achieve this success, what skills or abilities you had to use. Describe what you particularly like about each success, what makes it stand out in your mind.

Exercise 3. Feelings. Describe the best job you ever had. What did you like about it? Describe your worst job. Exactly what did you find so bad about it? Now take all that you have written, and from it make two lists, one of skills and one of desirable elements.

One way to make the analysis of these exercises more thorough is to do it with a friend. Each of you do the exercises by yourself and then read out your answers to the other; the listener can then help the reader fill in the lists from what she hears. Another person can often see many things that you can't. It is also hard for many people to talk of themselves in positive terms; your colleague can draw out from you the skills you may overlook in yourself. Below is a list.

Skills	*Desirable Elements*
Analyze	Being in charge
Communicate	Competition
Compile	Developing others
Coordinate	Doing good
Counsel	Fun
Create	Learning
Design	Money
Handle	New experience
Help	People
Innovate	Physical exercise
Lead	Recognition
Negotiate	Religious values
Operate	Security
Persuade	Status
Teach	Travel

Where Do You Want to Go?

Pulling together the two lists, you should now be able to write a description of your job objective—the type of job you would like to have *and* have shown you have the skills for. For the assistant, here are some of the possible choices:

1. Essentially same job as assistant
   Increased skill level
   Different type of industry or function
   Higher-level manager
2. Management
3. Specialized career outside of present job, such as sales or working with computers
4. Own business

I'd like to talk a bit about these choices. Most assistants will probably choose 1. This may be a mistake. You have spent time looking into yourself to discover what you are really suited to do. Don't put aside the "dreams" and come back to reality. If your personal job objective—the expression of what you really are—isn't anything like your present job, you must do some deep thinking about the time you spend in a job, how happy or unhappy you are in your present job, and how you can begin to approximate your ideal job.

THE FUTURE OF THE ASSISTANT

Even those of you who are choosing the role of an assistant as your ideal job must be aware that the job itself is changing. Because of the advent of word processing, many of the traditional jobs of the assistant are being removed.

If you remember, in the chapter on the role of the assistant, I said that some administrative assistants have the responsibility but not the title. Taking this fact into consideration, let's look at where a person with the title of "secretary" could move without essentially changing her role from that of an assistant.

WORD PROCESSING
↓

Correspondence Secretary	←	*Traditional Secretary/Assistant*	→	*Administrative Assistant to more than one manager*
Technician with expertise in word processing Prepares and edits text Can move up to supervisory position in word processing		Organizes boss Writes Types May supervise Has special duties		Arranges for work to be processed Prepares special reports

What seems to be happening in that the traditional assistant now has two routes to management-level work. The new administrative assistant working for a number of managers and concerned with the handling of special projects is at last a true member of the management team. On the other side, we have a person who is very competent in text preparation. That can be, in itself, an interesting and new career choice. She may want to move up to supervise other technicians. Both paths can lead today's assistant to management-level responsibility.

Other Routes to Management

The assistant who is not in an organization in which word processing has divided the work this finely but wants to move into a management position must look around the organization to see areas in which an assistant can succeed to a managerial job. She may already be in such a job. On the other hand, if her manager is an engineer and she has no engineering background, she could not succeed to his job. If her manager is in a personnel, administrative services, or credit area, where she could learn a lot of the job through experience and extra education, that type of move becomes plausible.

Some of you may have discovered in your self-analysis that you would prefer to spend your working life in a career other than that of an assistant or manager. Two fields I feel are excellent for women are sales and computers. The sales field is for the woman who likes to work independently and prefers her rewards to be commensurate with her work. In other words, the harder she works, the more money she makes. Some companies resist women in sales as they resist women in many other areas of the organization. Other companies have experienced the effectiveness that a woman's edge in people orientation can bring to their sales department.

The future of computer-wise people is fabulous. More and more functions in the organization are computerized and the need for people who are experts in this area will continue to grow. If you think you might like to get into this field, arrange to take an aptitude test at one of your local community colleges. You could take courses there at night.

There are, of course, many areas in which you might like to get involved. If this taste of career planning has convinced you that you're not sure where you want to go, but you do know you don't want to remain an assistant, I suggest you use either the Bolles or Crystal and Bolles book to explore the best job choice for you further.

Entrepreneurship may be the furthest possible career choice you see for yourself. But it is increasingly a choice of women who are willing to invest large risks for large rewards. Where do you "find" your own business? One way is to make a business out of a hobby. A kite store and an antique store are examples of this. Another way is to capitalize on a particular skill you have—a catering service, a furniture refinishing service, and a wedding advisory service are examples of this. Still another way is to line up with a partner who may have a particular skill while you have the organizing ability.

Whatever your focus, plan your entry into the world of business carefully. Take courses in running a small business. Plan not to make money for at least six months. Be careful of your cash flow. And take into account all expenses that go into your product or service when you are pricing.

SOME CASE HISTORIES

I collect life stories. When someone in a seminar tells me about a special approach to career success, I collect it so that I can pass it on to others. Here, I'd like to share two real-life stories with you. They are both about women who started as secretaries and are now in management.

Margaret is administrative services manager for a large computer service firm with branches across North America. She started in the company as a secretary to a vice-president. Margaret was an excellent secretary—so good, in fact, that her boss bragged about her abilities. Other managers in the company wished that their secretaries could learn the kinds of things Margaret knew. Could she—her manager suggested—teach them some of her system? "Of course," said Margaret, and she arranged some informal meetings with these other secretaries. The results were wonderful, but not enough. Could she do something on a more formal basis? "Of course," said Margaret, and she had it made part of her job description, with a commensurate salary change.

Margaret's secretarial seminars became well known in the company. Margaret, meanwhile, took some evening courses in areas that would increase her effectiveness as a teacher. Eventually Margaret was asked to create a brand-new position: Her job was to travel to all the branches and run training courses for the secretaries there. What title would she like? Training supervisor—that seemed reasonable. Margaret stayed in this job for a couple of years, until she felt it was time to move. She liked the company and wanted to stay there but she also liked the idea of moving up. So she looked for another supervisory position in the company that she could fill and that held promise for future promotion.

She settled on the administrative services area, an area into which she felt she could fit without too much adaptation. There was also a manager there who was known as a "mover" and would probably move up from his position in a few years. Margaret arranged a lateral transfer to a supervisory position in the administrative services area and did her usual excellent job. By the time the manager moved up, his job was hers.

Sandra's story had a lot to do with luck. At least that's what her "friends" said. Sandra was secretary to a middle manager in the head office of a very large utility. Being a good secretary, she excelled in her work and began to outgrow it. She asked for more responsibilities and got them. She handled that increased workload magnificently. She liked her job, but even with the new functions, it became routine. She wanted to be a manager. Sandra talked to her boss about it; he was sympathetic, would hate to lose her, but would keep challenging her and keep an eye out for opportunities. She talked to personnel. It would certainly take note of her goals and proven abilities when a suitable job came up. Still nothing.

Sandra was bored, so she began to get involved in the N.S.A. She became a member of the executive committee and had the opportunity there to develop her leadership skills. She liked it; she knew she'd make a good manager. The next year, when vacation time came around, Sandra decided to invest some time in studying herself. Perhaps she was going in the wrong direction. So she took a week and went off to a quiet resort to sit in the sun with some career planning books and work out her objectives. She looked at every aspect of herself and decided that she definitely wanted to be a manager.

Coming back from her vacation, she was a little depressed. But the first person who met her when she entered the office was a friend who said: "Sandra, are you lucky!" Sandra was bewildered until her friend explained. The personnel department was being expanded and Sandra was one of five people whose names had been suggested for the new supervisory position. Of course she got the job. Of course she did it well. And she is now looking around the company to see where her next step should be.

These stories illustrate the "hows" of career planning. These two successes were a combination of hard work, directed action, education, and an understanding of organizations. I'd like to summarize for you what I consider to be the most important elements in the "hows" of career planning.

GETTING-AHEAD GUIDELINES FOR WOMEN IN BUSINESS

General Principles

Work hard. But sensibly so. Work at being competent in the areas your company sees as important. Be successful in their eyes. Nine-to-fivers do not get ahead.

Love what you do. You will never be successful at something you hate. Some of my best ideas come on evenings and weekends. If my work were not such an important and satisfying part of my life, I wouldn't be open to its constant intrusion. Enthusiasm, energy, and innovativeness are all functions of this guideline.

Consider time your greatest resource. Time is the only completely egalitarian part of life. Everyone has exactly the same amount every day. People who achieve what they want in life squeeze out time for what they really want to do. I've always had the greatest respect for people who take evening courses. They spend the whole day working and struggle to stay awake at night to improve themselves. You have the time—but you have to use it well.

Set goals and record progress. Goals stretch a person. They give her direction and help her to focus her energies. Don't just set them; work on them. And assess your progress. If you're not moving as you thought you would, why not? Is the goal unreasonable? Or have your approaches been faulty?

Keep your work in synchronization with your total life. One of the things we women should *not* learn from men in business is their tendency in the past to relegate everything but their work to second place. Close relationships, children, friends, hobbies, sports, leisure can all be important refreshments and energizers that allow you to be even better at your job.

Be willing to risk. Women aren't known for their willingness to take risks. But we must change if we are to achieve more. If you won't risk taking on a new responsibility, learning to use new equipment, or even taking on a new job, you will never really know what you can achieve.

Organizational Principles

Make yourself visible. Sign your name. Get co-billing on reports. Introduce yourself to others by name, not as so-and-so's assistant. Write for the company newsletter. Sit on committees. This is the complement to hard work. You've got to let people know how good you are. Note how difficult it is to do this if you have internal messages about humility and modesty.

Get power. Or, if you can't have your own, ally yourself with it. One of the sources of power for you can be your expertise. It makes you important to your manager and the organization. You can also use the power of personal influence. It is easier for people to promote you if they like you. Your legitimate power is the power of your title. That's why title is so important. Who you are connected with also gives you power. If your manager is very influential in the organization, you can share in his power.

Find yourself a mentor. This can be, but doesn't have to be, your boss. A mentor is a guide—usually an experienced person in the organization who is willing to take a fledgling under wing to help that person develop. It doesn't have anything sexual about it. Men have been doing it with men for years. Showing you the ropes, giving shortcuts, introducing you to the right people are all ways the mentor can help you. What does the mentor get out of it? The reputation of being a developer and the chance to see his or her ideas carried on by someone else.

Play up your uniqueness. If you are the only woman in meetings, don't try to hide it. Play on the fact that you will be noticed and make yourself memorable for ability.

Join other women for support. It's difficult and stressful to try to get ahead. "Moral support" from other women can be a great aid to you. Other women can also be part of a mutual aid scheme. There's a lot of business done in the "old buddy network." And if women can't join them—as they often can't—they have to form their own helping groups.

Tune in to the organization. There are several ways to increase your rapport with the organization that will help you to get ahead.

1. Talk in organization terms. If the organization doesn't see intuition as a good reason for what you're proposing, make up a logical analysis that will be accepted.

2. Be a part of the team. Don't expend energy complaining about people; you will be seen as overly emotional. You don't have to like people to be able to work with them.

3. Study the personality and life-style of the organization. If it's on a fast track, you have to be, too, for success. If it's slow and conservative, that determines your approach, too.

CHOICES

To bring together all the career planning ideas I've been talking about, I'm going to draw you a picture. It is a picture of a typical secretary to a middle manager in a large corporation, and contains at least eight possible career routes for this secretary. (See Figure 8.)

Route 1 means increasing responsibility in her present job, perhaps with a change in title, and, of course, with a change in salary.

Routes 2 and 3 are moves to other assistant positions. Route 2 is to a different function either because she is interested in it or because it provides a better route to higher positions. Route 3 is a move to an assistant role at a higher level of the company.

Route 4 is moving into her manager's job. That's with all the provisions we've talked about.

Figure 8: Eight possible career routes for a secretary.

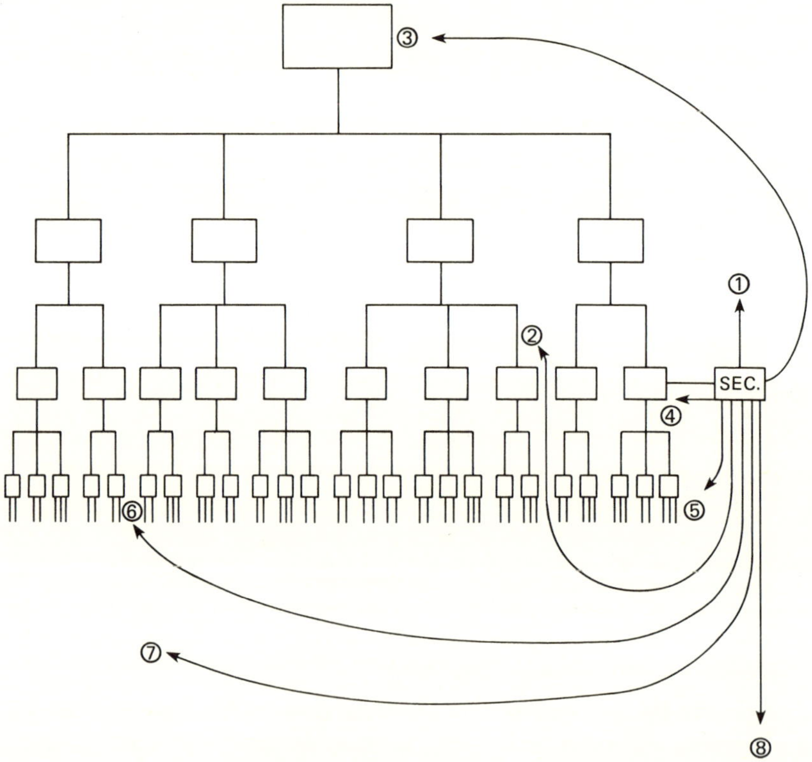

Routes 5 and 6 are part of the "one step backward, two steps forward" strategy. They are to line jobs either under her present manager or in another department; that other department could be a world processing unit, for example. These moves may even entail decreases in salary. The advantage of such moves, however, is that they eventually enable her to move upward, whereas she was stymied as an assistant.

Route 7 is outside the organization. This may be a good move if she feels she will never be seen as other than a secretary in that company. It could also be a way of getting different experience and a different title so that she can come back into the company on a new and better career path, or it could be a move to a specialized career.

Route 8 is to her own business. That route may seem the most farfetched, but if she has special talents and a lot of spunk it could be the only real one for her. Each of these paths has its own risks and its own rewards. Of course, the greater the risk, the greater the reward, and vice versa. In real life only you can decide the best way for you.

Throughout this chapter I have emphasized personal choice. This is because each of you is an individual in an individual situation. To get the most from your working life, you must be the person in charge. I sincerely hope you find your way.

11

SPECIAL PROBLEMS

or "What do I do in a situation like this?"

The following questions have been asked by people attending my seminars. I've chosen those that I think will be most helpful to the most people.

Question 1: How can I get out of the secretarial field if every time I go for an interview they insist on putting me there?

Answer: First, stop telling them you *are* a secretary. One of the reasons I think it is important for you to have a different title—administrative assistant, or assistant to, or assistant manager, or research specialist—is that these titles carry a different connotation from secretary. I'm not downgrading secretaries. I'm saying that if you want to do something different, your first step may be to get a different title.

Second, make out your résumé to reflect your skills and experience. Rather than saying "Acted as secretary to vice-president of personnel," say: "Assisted vice-president of personnel, including the following duties: interviewing of prospective employees; research and preparation of special reports, including one on absenteeism in the company; supervision of office staff, including selection and appraisal." You see? You're selling your skills, not a stereotyped position.

Third, persist in looking for a position that, if not exactly what you want, has a possibility of growth in it. Sometimes a young, small, fast-growing company will be the best. Sometimes it is a large corporation that is committed to internal advancement through job posting. Shop around.

Question 2: One of the office people I supervise is extremely negative. How can I change her?

Answer: I don't know if you can. You must realize that people don't necessarily act the way they do to "bug" you. They may do it because that action has proved to be useful in their lives. You come along and say: "Stop acting that way." It won't be easy for that person. I can, however, suggest three approaches you might take with her:

1. Start complimenting her. Talk to her only in positive terms. Give her attention only when she says something positive; otherwise try to ignore her. This action on your part may begin to turn her around because she will want attention, but you will give her that attention only for positive behavior. You're trying to get her to live with a substitution for her negativism.
2. Don't waste your energy. Learn to live with it. Laugh it off. Ignore it. The problem may not be her negativity; it may be your reaction to it.
3. If she's affecting those around her and you can't see her changing, you might try to ease her to another area of the company. Suggest to her that she seems unhappy here; what would she like to do about it? That may shake her up and make her realize what is happening. If not, you may be able to transfer the employee to another area, where she will be happier.

Question 3: How do I deal with the jealousy of others as I move up in the company? I've already lost some friends.

Answer: This is a difficult question for me to answer without seeming to be negative myself. You have to realize that nothing in life comes free; there is no "free lunch." To succeed in a career you must invest time, energy, and risk. You may also have to trade off some satisfactions for others. As part of that you may have to see some friends and acquaintances disappear as you move up. If, for example, you become supervisor to a group with whom you used to work, your new subordinates must learn to accept you in your new position because you *are* a different person—their leader. You have to make decisions on transfers, discipline, terminations, raises, and so forth that make it very difficult for you to maintain exactly the same relationship you once had with these people. You may have to settle for respect, not liking.

Question 4: I have a problem with one man for whom I work who has the habit of staring at my bust while talking to me. What can I do?

Answer: This can be considered a form of sexual harassment. You have a right not to be treated as a sexual object. How can you handle it? That depends on your own style of communication, your relationship to the person (a peer, your boss, the president of the company?), and what you want to accomplish. I think you *have* to do something for your own self-esteem. Realistically, the bigger the gap between the two of you in the organization hierarchy, the riskier action will be; that means there's a range of "soft" to "hard" answers:

1. Try to train the person to look you in the face: "John, I'd feel more comfortable if you looked me in the face rather than all around when we talk."
2. Use a direct, nonemotional question: "Is there something on my dress?"
3. Tell him directly: "I don't like you staring at my body when I talk to you."
4. Try reverse psychology. A number of women who had this problem tell me they stopped it by staring at the man's crotch. It cured him.

Question 5: A lot of people say that dress is very important in career advancement. How do you feel about that?

Answer: I think dress is important, but it must be seen in context. For example, I was driving through the city awhile ago and had stopped at a traffic light when I saw a woman standing at a bus stop. She was dressed in a very formal, pinstripe three-piece suit. She carried an attaché case rather than a pocketbook. A perfect example of the "dress for success" mode. *And she was chewing gum like a cow.*

I think women have to dress professionally. They also have to talk, act, and think professionally. Personally, I wear suits and dresses. Sometimes I wear close-toed shoes, sometimes open-toed. I like to wear colors that are becoming; I don't look good in banker's gray or navy blue.

What you have to look out for in dressing is coming across as a sex object. About a year ago a woman in one of my seminars told me she had a difficult problem. Being in sales, she was expected to take clients to lunch. But, she said, she was always being propositioned. I dealt with her problem from an assertiveness viewpoint—how she could go beyond the sexual innuendos and get back to the business.

I felt I had given her the best answer I could, but something bothered me about it. I only realized what it was a few days after the seminar was over. The woman was dressing in a way designed to encourage sexual advances. The first day of the seminar she had arrived in a jacket very tightly and oddly buttoned under the breast that emphasized her ample bust. The second day of the seminar she had worn a dress with a low neckline. And the third day she wore a clingy white wool. Unconsciously, I'm sure, she was actually encouraging the behavior she decried. Tailored suits would make a real difference in her career.

Question 6: My husband thinks all career women are hard, masculine types. I want to get ahead. How do I change his mind?

Answer: Introduce him to a few successful women. If they are anything like the ones I have met, they got where they are by being smart, charming, and very people oriented. As Barbara Walters has said: "The average lady tycoon is more feminine than the average housewife."

Realize, too, that your husband's opinion may only be an excuse on his part. What he may really be saying is, "I'm worried about how things are going to change for us as you move up in the company." If you have a commitment to the marriage, make sure you put some energy into that commitment as well as into your career. And realize that change in attitudes comes slowly.

One woman I recently met told me how difficult it had been five years before when she had gone back to work. Her husband and children refused to help with the housework and she found herself with two jobs—one at work and one at home. After about a month, she came home one night and declared that she wasn't going to do any more housework until she got some help. What happened? She said that her husband didn't talk to her for three months. How were things five years later? According to her: "Coming along—slowly."

A wife with a career is a source of discomfort for a lot of men. It takes time, lots of communication, and caring to get over attitudes. Those attitudes may have been instilled in your husband when he was a child.

Question 7: I think my boss is an alcoholic. I'm afraid he's going to lose his job. What can I do to help him?

Answer: It is very caring of you to want to help him but you are definitely limited in how much you can do. The most helpful thing—and the riskiest—is to tell your manager that people in the company are expressing dissatisfaction with his work. That may shock him into realizing the extent of his problem. He might also fire you out of anger.

I think *you* are the person you have to worry about if your boss is so incompetent you are missing out on what you can learn from a competent boss. In addition to—or instead of—telling your manager where his problem is leading him, you ought to start looking for a new position either in the same company or out of it. Otherwise, if and when he gets sacked, you may be sacked too.

Question 8: There are an increasing number of women managers. But I don't know how I'd like working for a woman. How do other assistants feel about this?

Answer: I find an increasing number of assistants who work for women. How do they like it? Many find it an advantage. Women bosses are often more understanding of personal needs. Because they have had to work hard to get where they are, they can be very supportive of an assistant's career aims. I think the "queen bee" that once epitomized the woman executive is disappearing.

But a woman boss can also be demanding. She may have to be better than any man in her place to stay there and, because of it, ask a lot from those around her. That can be a good learning experience for you and an opportunity to gain from her expertise and her example.

Question 9: My boss has asked me to represent him at a number of professional meetings. I've always refused because I'm afraid of speaking in front of a group. What can I do about this fear?

Answer: Lots. It's estimated that about 40 percent of people are afraid of public speaking. So you're not alone. Many women in particular have learned to be modest and quiet as part of their socialization. That may keep you from speaking up. The further up you go in management, the more you need to be able to speak to groups. So it's important to overcome the fear. Here are some suggestions:

1. Take a course in public speaking.
2. Join Toastmasters International, a nonprofit organization that teaches its members to make speeches. It is also a good place to meet other business people as part of "networking."
3. Ask yourself what it is about public speaking that bothers you. If it's a "message" about being humble, confront it with the reality of your career plans. If it's fear of a negative reaction, give yourself the edge of preparing well. I think preparation is about 80 percent of the effectiveness of a presentation. Know your subject inside out. Anticipate questions.
4. Practice. Although nervousness will never fully disappear, it will become more manageable. When I first started giving seminars five years ago, I usually spent a miserable weekend before each one with an upset stomach. That has disappeared, but my hands still shake the first morning—and that's with a schedule of 35 seminars a year. Think of nervousness as a way of revving up your body to do its best. You are more aware and alert because of the nervousness. And if you are well prepared and interested in your subject, your nervousness will quickly be lost in your own enthusiasm.

Question 10: My boss is a traditionalist but, in spite of the routine work, I enjoy working for the company. Should I be looking for a job with more responsibility?

Answer: No one can tell you what kind of job you should have. What you might want to do is analyze the relative pluses and minuses of the job you have now in relation to other jobs you might get. Try using a weighted pros and cons list to look at the relative merits of staying in this job or taking a new one. Write down the pros and cons of each of your choices. Assign a number to each item ranging from 1 (little or no importance) to 5 (great importance). See Table 2 for an example.

The other job gives you about the same number of pluses with fewer drawbacks. Such an analysis can help you to look at risk from a logical point of view. In this case the assistant should probably change her job. In your case it would depend on the elements and their relative importance in your own lists.

Table 2.

Present Job		*Other Job*	
Pros	*Cons*	*Pros*	*Cons*
+4 good salary	−4 routine	+4 promotion possibilities	−4 less money to start
+2 secure	−4 future	+4 more challenge	−1 getting used to people
+3 easy transportation			
+9	−8	+8	−5

Question 11: I have a subordinate who is not a very good worker. She's been with the company about 15 years and has been passed around a lot of departments. What can I do with her?

Answer: This is one of the most common questions I am asked in management seminars. A long line of supervisors unwilling to confront a poorly functioning employee end up with that employee 10, 15, or even 20 years later still being a poor worker and firmly entrenched in it. You have the same three choices in dealing with this employee as you had with your own manager: live with it, change it, leave (or have the employee leave). Your choice depends on the circumstances:

1. Live with it. How close is she to retirement? What effect does she have on the rest of the group? If your answers are soon and little, don't waste your energy.
2. Change it—or her. What are the probabilities of being able to change her habits? Has it been tried at all and what happened? Can she be scared into better work? Can she be rewarded into better work? The longer a person has lived with a certain way of doing things, the more motivation is necessary to get her to change.
3. Get her to leave. Does the company owe her for all these years? Can she be relegated to a minor position where she does little harm? Can she be transferred?

As a trainer I am in the business of changing people and I would opt for that as the ideal first step here. But it takes a lot of time and energy to change people; it's also not guaranteed. If your change management doesn't work, you have to move into 1 or 3. Many companies would be loath to fire her after all these years and she might also sue for unjust dismissal (probably all appraisal records say satisfactory). You will most likely end up either living with it or trying to get her into a relatively harmless position in the organization.

Learn from a situation like this. Don't give "average" appraisals across the board and then expect people to become good employees.

Question 12: Do you have any advice on the problems of "home work"? My husband and children expect me to do all the housework in addition to my job. I'm exhausted.

Answer: Of course you are. You could handle the problem by using some management techniques at home.

- Clarify the job descriptions. What exactly has to be done, how often, and by whom? Define daily, weekly, and monthly chores.
- Set standards. But don't set them too high. How clean does your house have to be?
- Delegate. To each according to ability and preference. In my house my son likes to wash floors. My daughter doesn't mind vacuuming. My husband hates garbage but will mow. When my mother visits she likes to cook. I enjoy cooking and shopping.
- Stress teamwork. Emphasize the goals of the family. Just as you are all sharing in the rewards of the family, you must all be responsible for the work.
- Monitor and appraise. Are the jobs being done? Well? Are there grievances? Handle them.
- Reward and reinforce. Have children earn their rewards by doing their work assignments. Your family can spend Saturday morning doing chores and then enjoy an afternoon out together.
- Hire experts when necessary. It may be worth it to you and your family to hire someone to do some of the work—a cleaning lady, a neighborhood boy to mow the lawn—or to go out and get a restaurant meal.

Question 13: What's the best way to ask for a raise?

Answer: Carefully—and with preparation. If you feel you deserve a raise, there are a number of things you should do before you talk to the boss about it.

1. Decide how much you want. Be prepared to talk within a range of salary but also be clear on the minimum you will settle for. If you are clear in your mind on what you are worth, you will automatically communicate that firm purpose when you talk to your manager.
2. Prepare a short presentation on your abilities. You want to be able to show your manager how your worth to the department has increased to warrant this raise.
3. Decide what you will do if you don't get the raise. Will you leave? Will you settle for a substitute, like some kind of perk? Will you defer the raise for a stated period of time?

When you are ready to ask for the raise, keep these points in mind:

1. Choose a good time, like right after a successful project that has put both you and the department in a good light.
2. Use assertiveness techniques: I-talk and broken record to persist in your point of view; listening and stroking to make your manager comfortable.
3. Bargain. Ask for more than your minimum so that you can negotiate with your boss.

Question 14: Do you ever have male assistants in your seminars? What are they like and do they fit into the seminar?

Answer: The first time a male assistant attended one of my assistants' seminars, I opened the meeting by welcoming our "token man." He took it laughingly, as I intended he should. I've had about four male assistants in these seminars. Three of them found the material just as useful as the women did. Although, as men, they may get more general respect in the organization, their roles as assistants are still nebulous. Whether a male or a female holds the assistant's job, each must find his or her own "clout" in expertise and good interpersonal skills.

The fourth man was difficult. He was very aggressive and outspoken. I can handle that, because I often teach male managers. But, to my surprise, I found that all the women in the room hung on his every word. Whenever he had an opinion, no one would contradict him. It was an example of how women may be barriers to themselves; by constantly deferring to a male they make themselves inferior.

Question 15: I was promoted to assistant supervisor two months ago. I'm having a terrible time being accepted by my former peers. Should it take this long?

Answer: Or longer. My experience with people moving into supervisory roles of any kind is that they have unrealistic expectations about the settling-in process. A new supervisor will think before she moves up that things will automatically change once she gets the title. Of course, that's not so.

We've looked at leadership as an earned position; because it is, your new subordinates are looking at your behavior in your new position and deciding how and when they will accept your leadership. In general, those moving into a supervisory role have told me it took them anywhere from three months to a year to establish themselves. Of course, if you use your management skills, the time can be on the shorter side. And some ineffective supervisors never get accepted at all. Keep working at being the best you can in your position. Show your former co-workers that you are an able leader.

Also, watch out for the "old buddy" syndrome. It's very common for supervisors who are moved up to a supervisory position over former co-workers to experience this. The "old buddy" syndrome refers to a tendency on the part of the new supervisor to try to continue to be a buddy to former co-workers and to be a supervisor at the same time. It usually doesn't work.

Question 16: It's been my experience that women are sometimes the worst enemies of other women. Why do they have to be so bitchy?

Answer: Many women have difficulty with so-called male chauvinists; we've looked at the reasons for that. But many women in business also experience difficulties with other women. It seems ironic, doesn't it? They're the ones who should most understand and help.

It's a real source of sadness to me that women have such a bad reputation for backbiting, vindictiveness, and general nonhelping behaviors to other women. I have been helped by both men and women in my career; I have also experienced women's negative behavior. In five years of seminars, to almost 6,000 men and women, every one of whom evaluated my seminars, I have received only two evaluations I considered personally offensive, both of these from women.

To deal with this problem of women's behavior, we need to understand the source of it. I've already referred, earlier in the book, to the "kick the cat" syndrome. I feel that when women are hateful toward other women, it's primarily because of their latent frustration and rage. As Rollo May has so aptly put it, "Power corrupts and powerlessness corrupts completely." People, including women, who are relatively satisfied with their growth and rewards in the business world can afford to be generous with others. But a majority of women feel underused, put down, and generally discriminated against; such feelings must have an outlet and, unfortunately, it seems to come out against their weaker sisters.

What I'm saying, of course, is that women are not naturally of a "mean" and inferior nature. It's circumstances that cause this negative behavior. As things improve for women, they will not have to express their frustrations through such behavior.

Question 17: You also teach male supervisors and managers in some of your seminars. What do they think of their assistants?

Answer: Ironically, not what the assistants think of themselves. The misperceptions and miscommunications that managers and their assistants have are enormous. I'll give you an example.

One of the biggest problems that assistants bring into my seminars is that they don't have enough responsibility delegated to them by their managers; they want more. On the other hand, managers experience one of their biggest problems in time management. When I discuss this subject with a group of managers and we come to delegation as one of the best means of improving time use, I usually suggest that they delegate more to their assistants. Too often I hear "Oh, she doesn't want any more responsibility. She's happy just typing and filing." These people aren't talking to each other.

Throughout this book, I've stressed opening up communication about things that are not going right for you. Don't assume that your manager is purposely holding back on you if you haven't sat down with him and talked about your aims. You might be surprised to find him quite happy to delegate some of his responsibilities to you.

Question 18: I find that one of the most difficult parts of my job as an assistant is introducing change to the office staff. I've had to bring in new machines, new procedures, new forms, and so on. It's a struggle to get people used to them. Can you give me any hints to make it easier?

Answer: Change is difficult, to some extent, for most people. It can also make work exciting and challenging. The key to introducing change lies in recognizing both these aspects. To introduce change effectively, you have to be willing to accept people's feelings and even resistance, to help them work through these. You also want to make the change experience interesting. I suggest:

1. Give them the facts. Don't tell them it's going to be as easy as one, two, three if it isn't. You can paint something in positive terms without lying to people: "The new procedure will take some time to learn; we don't expect you to know how to follow it overnight. And I think you'll find it eventually makes your work much easier."
2. Accept people's feelings: "I realize it will take some time to get used to it." "Of course it was easier with a system you had used for five years." "It's awkward at first, I know."
3. Get people involved in the change process. Where will we put the new machine? How can we best use it? How can we schedule training on it? Any suggestions on how to improve its use?
4. Reinforce the change process. Give feedback on even small successes: "You're really picking up speed on that." "You followed these procedures right to the letter. Thank you for doing it so carefully." "I see you're using the new form. It looks good, doesn't it?"
5. Periodically bring about change that the staff is looking for. If it sees change as something always being "laid on" it, it will resist. Be open to changes the staff suggests that can be implemented. Change will then be seen as part of the job and as something pleasant.

SELECTED READING LIST

These books are arranged by subject matter so you can find the titles you are most interested in quickly. Books that have been put out in paperback versions are noted with a (P). This bibliography contains only books I personally found useful that would give good value for the time spent in reading them.

The Woman in Business

Cannie, Joan K., *The Woman's Guide to Management Success*. Englewood Cliffs, N.J.: Prentice-Hall, 1979.

Halas, Celia, and Matteson, Roberta, *I've Done So Well—Why Do I Feel So Bad?* New York: Ballantine Books, 1979. (P)

Harragan, Betty L., *Games Mother Never Taught You*. New York: Warner Books, 1977. (P)

Jongeward, Dorothy, and Scott, Dru, *Women as Winners*. Reading, Mass.: Addison-Wesley, 1976.

Smith, Genevieve, *Genevieve Smith's Deluxe Handbook for the Executive Secretary*. Englewood Cliffs, N.J.: Prentice-Hall, 1979.

Trahey, Jane, *Women and Power*. New York: Avon Books, 1977. (P)

Williams, Lucille G., *The New Executive Woman*. New York: Mentor Books, 1977. (P)

Human Relations and Communications

Baer, Jean, *How to Be an Assertive (Not Aggressive) Woman*. New York: Signet, 1976. (P)

Butler, Pamela E., *Self-Assertion for Women*. San Francisco: Harper & Row, 1976.

Du Brin, Andrew J., *Human Relations: A Job-Oriented Approach*. Reston, Va.: Reston Publishing, 1978.

Dyer, Wayne W., *Your Erroneous Zones*. New York: Avon Books, 1976. (P)

Fensterheim, Herbert, and Baer, Jean, *Don't Say Yes When You Want to Say No*. New York: Dell, 1975. (P)

Flesch, Rudolph, *On Business Communications: How to Say What You Mean in Plain English*. New York: Barnes & Noble, 1974.

James, Muriel, and Jongeward, Dorothy, *Born to Win*. Reading, Mass.: Addison-Wesley, 1971.

Massey, Morris, *The People Puzzle*. Reston, Va.: Reston Publishing, 1979.

Nierenberg, Gerald, and Calero, Henry H., *How to Read a Person Like a Book*. New York: Cornerstone Library, 1971.

Smith, Manuel J., *When I Say No, I Feel Guilty*. New York: Bantam, 1975. (P)

Time Management

Bliss, Edwin C., *Getting Things Done*. New York: Bantam, 1976. (P)

Douglass, Merrill, *The Time Management Workbook*. Grandville, Mich.: Time Management Center, 1978.

Lakein, Alan, *How to Get Control of Your Time and Your Life*. New York: Signet, 1973. (P)

MacKenzie, R. Alec, *The Time Trap*. New York: AMACOM, 1972.

Supervision

Bittel, Lester R., *What Every Supervisor Should Know*, 3rd ed. New York: McGraw-Hill, 1974.

Imundo, Louis V., *The Effective Supervisor's Handbook*. New York: AMACOM, 1980.

Sartain, A. Q., and Baker, A. W., *The Supervisor and the Job*. New York: McGraw-Hill, 1978.

Career Planning

Bolles, Richard N., *What Color Is Your Parachute?* Berkeley, Calif.: Ten Speed Press, 1972.

Crystal, John C., and Bolles, Richard N., *Where Do I Go from Here with My Life?* Berkeley, Calif.: Ten Speed Press, 1974.

Gunther, Max, *The Luck Factor*. New York: Ballantine Books, 1977. (P)

Souerwine, Andrew H., *Career Strategies—Planning for Personal Achievement*. New York: AMACOM, 1978.

Miscellaneous

Arnold, John D., *Make up Your Mind*. New York: AMACOM, 1978.

Bachner, Jane, and Stone, Janet, *Speaking Up*. New York: McGraw-Hill, 1977.

Jones, William M., and Jones, Ruth A., *Two Careers, One Marriage*. New York: AMACOM, 1980.

INDEX